THE APARTMENT PLAYBOOK

24 YEARS OF INSIDER SECRETS

6 States • 43 Assets • 6,933 Units

Baron Saterbak, CAPS, CAM

Baron (left) and Gary Saterbak (right), circa 1995, at a new construction site in Battle Creek, Michigan.

Table of Contents

YOUR MULTIFAMILY PLAYBOOK

Multifamily real estate has become a cornerstone for investors seeking stability and long-term growth. *THE APARTMENT PLAYBOOK, 24-YEARS OF INSIDER SECRETS,* is an essential resource for anyone navigating this multifaceted field, from beginner investors to seasoned asset managers. This guide unravels the complexities of managing multifamily assets, equipping you with both the practical knowledge and strategic insights necessary to maximize the value of your properties and optimize your investment outcomes.

Structured in two parts that merge into each other, the book opens with a comprehensive overview of the key principles and best practices in multifamily asset management. Topics covered include effective property management, financial analysis, leasing strategies, tenant retention, risk management, and long-term capital planning. Each chapter provides actionable steps, expert advice, and industry insights, making it easy to understand and apply these concepts in real-world scenarios.

The second part of the book dives into an in-depth case study that illustrates the real-life application of these asset management principles. You'll gain insight into the day-to-day nuances and strategic thinking required in multifamily asset management through detailed analysis and breakdowns of decisions, challenges, and solutions. This case study not only brings theoretical concepts to life but also highlights the potential pitfalls and success factors in managing multifamily properties effectively.

Whether you're responsible for a single property or a portfolio, this book emphasizes the importance of strategic planning and operational efficiency. With its accessible style and comprehensive approach, this guide demystifies the complexities of the multifamily real estate sector. Key takeaways include how to assess property performance, identify areas for improvement, and leverage data-driven insights to inform decisions, ensuring sustainable asset growth.

This book is an indispensable tool for anyone looking to build expertise in multifamily asset management, offering both foundational knowledge and an insider's look at the strategies that drive success in one of the most dynamic sectors of real estate.

FROM RISK TO REWARD

2021 was a very good year. We made a strategic decision at the end of 2020 to liquidate our entire portfolio of properties. We closed the sale of our portfolio in May of 2021 and escaped the resulting carnage of the following years created by rapid debt rate expansion in 2022.

After completing the sale of our portfolio, I was burned out from working seven days a week for years. I decided to take some time off and write this book.

We had just completed navigating COVID, which generated extensive tenant delinquency, eviction bans, travel restrictions, office limitations, touring limitations, operational adjustments in technology, and centralization. The industry had become flooded with market participants who had limited background in the multifamily industry and were underwriting acquisition targets utilizing irresponsible and unreliable projections. The risk/reward proposition had compressed to levels that were not prudent for our capital or our investors' capital.

There are no guarantees in real estate, and over the next few years, that will become glaringly apparent as the market reels from high-leverage transactions with floating and fixed-rate debt.

However, as you will soon find out, the methods in this

book worked for me. With the outline and background this book provides, it is my hope that you will have a sound foundation to reach your financial and real estate goals. The rest will be up to you. This is an uphill battle from the beginning. Even an investment advisor will tell you that real estate is risky and should never be more than 10% of your portfolio. I love multifamily real estate. People need a place to live. That will never go away.

A cutthroat industry plagued with fraud and inexperience has caused property values to exceed reasonable investment criteria. Rising interest rates, combined with inflation and COVID, have put some operators out of business. The opportunity created by market cycles, greed, and uncontrollable expense increases can allow someone else's mistake to become your opportunity.

There are over one trillion in both floating and fixed-rate commercial real estate loans maturing in 2025. Many of these properties are multifamily whose current value is less than senior debt. These assets will be repriced to current market conditions and be opportunistic acquisition opportunities. Many historical sponsors will be precluded from participating in this market opportunity because they have or will default on existing property debts in 2023-2025.

The agency debt generally carries a term of 5 to 12 years. Shorter term acquisition bridge debt has terms of 5 years or less. That means the maturing loans are at interest rates near half of where current interest rates are today. The reality is there are literally hundreds of billions of dollars of bad real estate debt in the capital markets. The world of extend and pretend is coming to an end.

UNLOCKING MULTIFAMILY POTENTIAL

"Never invest in a business you cannot understand."

—Warren Buffett

Multifamily asset management plays a major role when it comes to the real estate industry, as it ensures efficient operation and maximization of value for multifamily properties. Welcome to *THE APARTMENT PLAYBOOK, 24-YEARS OF INSIDER SECRETS.*

This comprehensive guide will provide you with an in-depth exploration of the strategies, best practices, and important tools needed to succeed in this complex field. The multifamily sector demands expertise in areas such as property operations, financial performance, tenant relations, and market analysis. Effective asset management can drive long-term profitability, improve property value, and enhance investor returns. In today's ever-evolving real estate market, staying informed on regulatory changes, technological advancements, and shifting tenant preferences is paramount.

At the heart of every successful multifamily investment

lies the tenant. Tenants are the lifeblood of a property, a truth I learned at an early age. When I was just 13, I began pulling quarters from laundry machines and interacting with tenants. Those simple exchanges taught me that happy tenants are paying tenants, and building strong relationships with them can lead to stable, long-term occupancy. By the time I could drive, I knew many of the tenants by name. These experiences cemented the importance of tenant relations in property management and helped me understand how personal connections can transform a property.

As I matured, so did my exposure to the realities of commercial real estate. The cyclical nature of the industry, across multiple cycles, required me to quickly learn how to mitigate short and long-term risks. From understanding market fluctuations to navigating operational challenges, these lessons became foundational to my approach to asset management.

But first, let me tell you why I wrote this book.

I am Baron Saterbak. I am a real estate professional with over two decades of experience in multifamily operations, acquisitions, renovation, due diligence, and asset management for third-party owners, managers, and lenders.

I wrote this book because there is no better school for the multifamily commercial real estate sector than experience. Sometimes, it's a school of hard knocks with unforeseen market adjustments, annual federal, state, and local policy changes, operational adjustments, and ever-changing debt facilities. Recently, people have contacted me for my expertise regarding multifamily underwriting, due diligence, operational nuances, and renovation scope, prompting me to write this book.

This is a practical text drawn from twenty years of hands-on experience. It is intended to allow for an understanding of the multifamily process and assist in making sound investing decisions. In my experience, no "one size fits all" multifamily transaction exists. Each transaction, owner, management company, and lender have different criteria, goals, and motivations. I hope my thoughts and mistakes, along with this case study and transaction milestone, help teach anyone looking to expand into the apartment space.

Most people in the multifamily sphere have a sense of proprietary sauce. What makes them the best? It could be their brand "Company Name on (Street Name)," their renovation style, professionalism, or the return to their investors. However, everyone believes some part of it is in their underwriting. It isn't; it's the attention to on-site operations. I am confident anyone can learn how to execute a multifamily transaction with the proper guidance, effort, and willingness to pivot. I hope the presentation of this case study and the sharing of my knowledge can improve the industry and reduce risk in future multifamily transactions going forward.

I will provide examples of reports, documents, and financial analyses throughout the book. In doing so, I aim to include a wide range of explanations and some complex topics. Unless otherwise noted, the Phoenix MSA is where market and financial expertise are based, and the case study will be over a C asset in a C location. The country's markets, sub-markets, and regions vary in expenses, taxes, median income, and investor return expectations.

Quickly dissecting a multifamily transaction is an integral and undervalued skill. Passive investors frequently make investment decisions based on a sponsor's track record or a pitch deck. Being able to independently verify returns across different markets, business plans, financing structures, operational strengths, and horizons will allow you to identify the diamonds from the coal.

If this is your first multifamily transaction, that's okay, effective asset management is the first step for maximizing the value and returns of any multifamily transaction. Whether you are a real estate investor, a student, or a professional seeking to enhance your understanding, this guide will help you with the tools and confidence needed to succeed.

Before we begin, let me tell you that this book is not

based on research or classes. It is based on twenty years of onsite multifamily asset management as a key principal, managing partner, general partner, limited partner, passive investor, and consultant. Many people and companies have been directly and indirectly involved in shaping the opportunities and experiences over the years.

So, let us start this journey by understanding repositioning sponsorship:

Multifamily asset sponsorship consists of identifying and acquiring properties while implementing strategic improvements to improve their value and generate higher returns. This approach targets properties with potential for enhancement through renovations, operational efficiencies, and best business practices. Sponsors execute their envisioned business plan, often sourcing debt, providing loan guarantees, and overseeing renovations while backstopping cost overruns. They also ensure the property achieves the desired financial performance while giving a necessary track record for all stakeholders to be comfortable investing in the transaction.

Sponsors can be termed as the main driving force behind executing the business plan and effectively communicating with the lending facility, the ownership group, and the management team to achieve the investment goals. They can multiply property value and rental income by making long-term targeted improvements and effectively guiding the property's management. This approach also positions the property competitively in the market by upgrading amenities and improving operational efficiencies, thereby attracting and retaining tenants more effectively.

Investment growth is another significant benefit of multifamily sponsorship. This strategy can transform underperforming assets into high-performing institutional investments, offering investors substantial upside potential. Knowing and acquiring properties with untapped potential for value enhancement is a critical component of this approach, as is implementing strategic renovations to improve the property's appeal and functionality.

Operational efficiency is one of many ways to minimize costs, increase occupancy, and optimize revenue. Asset management entails improving property management practices and conducting detailed financial analyses of project returns, planning for financing, and budget management. Additionally, effective risk management is needed when it comes to identifying and mitigating risks associated with renovations and market changes so the investment remains sound.

In multifamily sponsorship, value creation extends beyond physical renovations; strategic market positioning is equally crucial. Sponsors typically begin by conducting comprehensive market research to understand tenant demographics, preferences, and local demand patterns. This insight enables sponsors to align renovations and operational improvements with market needs, targeting upgrades that tenants find most valuable, such as improved community spaces, high-speed internet, and smart home features. By understanding these elements, sponsors ensure that the enhancements resonate with potential tenants, justifying potential rent increases and supporting a high occupancy rate.

Sponsors also focus on tenant experience, which directly impacts tenant retention and the overall value of the property. Implementing efficient tenant management systems and offering online portals for rent payment, maintenance requests, and tenant communication creates a streamlined experience, reducing administrative burdens and fostering positive tenant relations. Happy tenants are more likely to renew leases, reducing turnover and stabilizing income, both of which make the property more attractive to potential future buyers.

Creating sustainable practices within the property can provide additional financial and operational benefits. Many sponsors are now incorporating eco-friendly upgrades, such as energy-efficient windows, appliances, and water-saving fixtures. These changes not only lower utility costs but can also appeal to environmentally conscious tenants. Beyond cost savings, these green improvements may also make the property eligible for various tax incentives or rebates, further enhancing returns. Energy-efficient properties are increasingly favored by investors as they align with broader environmental, social, and governmental trends in the investment community, which can positively influence the property's long-term market appeal and value.

Capital structuring is another area in which sponsors play a vital role. They identify and secure financing options that align with the property's business plan and anticipated returns. This can include options such as short-term bridge loans, traditional mortgages, or refinancing strategies. By tailoring the capital structure to the needs of the asset and market conditions, sponsors can optimize leverage, potentially enhancing returns for equity holders. This structured approach to financing, coupled with active cost management, helps sponsors maintain cash flow during renovations and ensures that they have sufficient resources to complete the project as planned.

Effective project oversight during renovation phases is critical to maintaining both timelines and budgets. Sponsors who closely monitor the renovation process, regularly assessing contractors' progress and quality, guarantee that improvements meet both operational standards and tenant expectations. Any delays or unexpected costs can jeopardize returns, so sponsors often have contingency funds and backup plans in place to mitigate risks.

Finally, sponsors remain involved in the exit strategy of the investment. Timing the sale to align with peak market conditions, particularly after renovations have maximized the property's value, is key to achieving strong returns. A well-prepared exit strategy may also involve preparing the property's financials, tenant records, and operational data to present a clear picture of its profitability and potential to future buyers. This attention to detail can command higher sale prices and attract more serious buyers, making the final stages of the investment as successful as the initial acquisition and renovation phases.

By focusing on these components, sponsors can transform properties, deliver substantial returns to investors, and contribute to the growth of their investment portfolios. The following chapters will delve deeper into each aspect, providing practical insights and strategies for successful multifamily sponsorship.

CHAPTER 1

From Vision to Value

"For a successful multifamily transaction, you must execute two out of three things: purchase right, operate right, and sell right."

Underwriting is all about collecting and organizing the financial information needed to project income, expenses, and investment returns, also known as a "Proforma." These projections guide decisions related to the purchase, sale, refinance, and repositioning of the potential asset. Underwriting is also the stage at which you can formulate a business plan for the apartment complex.

You can choose a General Partnership (GP), Limited Partnership (LP), partnership structures, or a more complex capital stack, potentially including preferred equity, mezzanine debt, or Tenants in Common (TIC) structure to accommodate a 1031 Exchange. Lastly, underwriting can give you an understanding of your current asset value. *Would you buy your assets today for that value or return? Can your equity be deployed at a higher return somewhere else?*

Underwriting also aims to make educated assumptions based on market and industry experience to create clarity for future analysis. Understanding an asset's underwriting is more meaningful than its location, condition, and sub-market median household income. While those factors are important, they do not make a property a worthwhile asset for your money machine.

For example, the location, condition, and household income become irrelevant when a 1970s property sells for $230k per unit, and new construction can be completed for roughly $245k per unit in 2024. Why would you buy a property over 50 years old for nearly the cost of a new one? This is a gross simplification of the larger analysis as new construction carries entitlement, architectural, and construction timelines that extend beyond the general repositioning renovation horizon.

A comprehensive underwriting process prevents shortsighted mistakes, and a conservative approach will allow you to turn singles into triples. Instead of making decisions based on a pitch deck or a shiny resume, underwriting lets you weed out any emotion to determine if the asset makes sense for your investor pool or individual investment criteria.

Remember that you cannot set your investment criteria in a bubble. We all need guidance and perspective from others in the industry. Target returns and criteria change with market conditions, cost of equity, and debt facilities. There are a few ways to set or know these criteria:

First, ask your ownership group what their goal is for their investment. In some cases, an investor group will give you criteria. Some ownership groups require cash flow, some require tax benefits, while others seek long-term equity growth or estate planning. Discussing your investment groups' criteria can prove beneficial to finding the right asset.

As an example, some groups are looking for a minimum of 150 units, built after 2000, with 9-foot ceilings and a washer and dryer in the unit. Their investment criteria can also require 5% Cash on Cash Return (CoC) and a projected 15% Internal Rate of Return (IRR).

However, in most cases, you will determine what the market will tolerate by submitting a Letter of Intent (LOI) on prospective purchases. A multifamily transaction usually occurs when need or greed exceeds the individuals' risk tolerance. Each part of the country has assumptions for the Capitalization Rate (CAP) and valuations.

Coastal California may generally trade around a 4 CAP plus or minus half a percent, while the sunbelt state, like Arizona, may trade at a 6 CAP with the same variance. In the Midwest, generally called the "flyover states," Ohio, for example, will trade around a 7.5 CAP plus or minus 1%.

Using a return that is too high on behalf of your investors can price you out of a specific market. You may have to lower your offers to achieve a higher return to your equity group. If you use a low return, you may accomplish those low returns, and in the worst case, you could lose everything. I will get into timing the market later, but I encourage you to always be optimistic and cautious, underwriting on the conservative side.

For our data, we will use a property in Phoenix, Arizona, a location generally accepted at the time as the fifth-largest market in the country. Before the 2008 financial crisis, Phoenix relied on a single industry: *construction* (A relatively brief history of development in Phoenix, n.d.).

Due to the tremendous economic growth since then, the total economic drivers now include two of the country's largest colleges as well as booming medical, industrial, technological, entertainment, and sports industries. Today investors view Phoenix as a resistant market, and due to continued job growth and economic drivers, the long-term horizon for Phoenix is bright. In some cases (determined by each market), some investor groups are willing to receive lower returns.

Blueprint for Success

If you do not already have an underwriting model to work from, there is nothing to be worried about, as you can always make them as complex or simple as you would like. You may feel like this is an impossible task. Know that it's worth all the effort. For example, when you are the one programming your assumptions and calculations, it gives an intimate understanding of each process step, model, and output.

All models are different, and there are no right or wrong formulas, but it is helpful to use a model you are familiar with and understand its formulas. When I started creating our underwriting model, it was a single-page Excel spreadsheet. Over the years, it has grown to over 10 tabs, including renovation schedules and a monthly business plan breakdown.

While the actual creation of a model is outside the content of this book, I will give examples, figures, and diagrams of some models. I highly recommend you find or download as many models as possible and manipulate their formulas and data. Moreover, comparing models will allow you to see different styles, formats, repetitive formulas, and data points. There are many free and paid options available across the internet. YouTube can also help you.

Once you are comfortable with a model, checking your model against another credible source must be your next step. Using multiple models will allow you to see variations in the resulting outputs. Some models use exact numbers, while others use rounding criteria. Even a minor difference in a calculation can vary a projection drastically. You will also see that, at times, underwriting can feel like keeping the tip of a fishing pole still while trying to meet your investor criteria.

I've used the same data across two different models and arrived at IRRs of 17% and 19%, respectively. While one IRR is better, that doesn't necessarily mean the model itself is more accurate. Small adjustments to a few inputs in an underwriting model can significantly alter loan amounts, CoC projections, and IRRs.

After you have reviewed some models, you can begin disassembling and adjusting them as needed. Incorporate the aspects that you find helpful for each model into your own. Your model will change as you become more familiar with your market and everyday situations.

Once you've gained confidence in customizing models, focus on refining variables specific to your property type and target market. Testing different scenarios within your model can reveal the impact of fluctuating rent rates, vacancy, and expense trends on projected returns. Adding sensitivity analysis tabs will allow you to observe the effects of these changes in real-time. An adaptable model that considers worst-case and best-case scenarios will offer more reliable insights and better risk management. Over time, these insights will enhance your predictive accuracy, offering you a robust tool that evolves with market conditions and your investment strategy.

When building your model, consider including a monthly proforma. Annual calculations are just too simplified, and it's challenging to determine rounding errors. Over time, you will develop confidence in a particular model. Putting 100 properties through an underwriting model is just the beginning of this journey.

High-Level Essentials

Did you know that multifamily asset sponsorship is a unique math puzzle combined with an overzealous art project?

Yes, as an investor, you rely on the sponsor and their team to execute the projected business plan. It would be best if you focused on their team and their track record. It is important to understand how they manage assets in their portfolio. The best way to do this is to call current or previous investors, management companies, or third-party vendors. Ask if the returns were as initially underwritten, if the management company pushed rents during ownership, and if the vendors received checks on time.

You might be wondering who your sponsor can be. A sponsor can come from anywhere, someone who was a broker, loan originator, or handyman. Anyone who can raise the equity needed for a transaction and is willing and able to sign for the debt and execute the projected business plan can be a sponsor. That is why it is so vital that you are aware of who you may be investing in. Remember, it isn't their money; it's yours, and you always have the potential to lose your investment.

When you take someone's money for investment in a multifamily transaction, you are taking on a fiduciary responsibility. Sometimes, people do not treat it that way. You can be managing someone's life savings, their child's education, or the generational wealth most seek to attain.

Often, sponsors provide a pitch deck in conjunction with the property offering and, with luck, their previous track record. Sometimes, these can be misleading. In most cases, they may not list unfavorable transactions, or perhaps they have listed assets they are not in operational control over but have a favorable return or passive interest.

I have seen a recent sponsor group founded by a previous real estate broker. In their track record, their passive investments were listed as an earlier transaction even though they were a silent, non-managing partner. The broker had invested 50k in another sponsored transaction but was not involved in any management activity, thus a passive investor.

The best evidence is to compare the underwriting at acquisition with the track record results, if possible. After a few case studies, including this one, you may find that solid returns can result from a rising rent market and a lower-than-projected exit CAP rather than expertise and best business practices. However, this does not diminish the need for an experienced sponsor; it exacerbates the issue.

Different sponsorship groups have various levels of control over individual transactions. Companies nationwide have succeeded in using either a third-party management company or a sponsor-operated and vertically integrated in-house management. The groups holding management in-house can exert additional control while making efficient and timely capital improvement decisions. Third-party companies can take an extended time to convince ownership of asphalt repairs or a renovation plan.

A third-party management company can allow a sponsorship group to focus on the acquisition and growth of a portfolio. Those with internal management teams can struggle to keep up with expansion, pulling their best staff to new assets. Usually, the sponsor has no personal on-site experience and relies entirely on third-party or internal management teams.

On average, the property will pay the management company 3-5% of Effective Gross Income (EGI), a relatively small number compared to its corporate expenses, including regional staff, human resources, accounting, and training. Without those centralized corporate support components, any multifamily asset will eventually suffer.

Owners and investors aim to maximize revenue and reduce expenses, but third-party managers can have other motivating factors. If two assets, for example, are struggling and owned by different groups, the management company may send more qualified staff to the property with the preferred ownership group. Third-party management companies operate for a fee, as indicated above, and usually hold no ownership percentage in the asset. Suppose you are investing in an internal, vertically integrated, sponsor-managed project. In that case, the ownership group may utilize staff for another asset benefit, leaving your property to suffer or having a less qualified on-site team member.

While we are all working together to accomplish the business plan, always keep in mind that not every stakeholder has your ownership group's best interests at heart. It requires your drive to push them to the business plan goals. Remember, a management company primarily focuses on the EGI, so they have little incentive to minimize your expenses above the Net Operating Income (NOI) or below Capital Expenses (CapX). It's always easier to replace a refrigerator than repair it, but it isn't always economical.

While this can be a concern in most cases, my favorite thing about multifamily assets is that you usually have 30 days to solve a problem. Time is always a deal killer; the faster you can do something, the better. But unforeseen things will always occur, and having 30 days to solve those items, like accounts payable, receivable, occupancy markers, staff turnover, or capital expenses is a gift.

Once you have determined you are content with the sponsorship and management groups, you must understand the team's capabilities more deeply. Try to answer these types of questions:

- Does the management company have enough staff, or will they need to bring in new talent?
- What is their employee turnover?
- What type of recruiting do they do?

While these tend to be a lesser factor, it is needed to understand who is operating your multimillion-dollar investment.

Take note of the sponsors' reporting criteria. Some sponsors, like Bear Holdings Group, provide quarterly physical property inspection reports to investors and management to ensure they maintain the physical asset according to best business practices. These reports will usually include details about grills on patios, irrigation leaks, disabled vehicles, trip hazards, and other liability items that the on-site team might overlook.

Attentive reporting can catch items quickly and allow for a proactive long-term approach to maintaining the physical assets instead of a reactionary one driven by outside factors. Generally, the on-site focus is prospect conversion and resident retention. Rarely is it the long-term outlook of the physical asset.

Second, how is the transaction structured? We will address this further throughout this book, but in most cases, factors include aligning common investment goals, structured fees, Preferred Return (Pref), and sponsor co-invest. Sometimes, a sponsor will add a Mezzanine Debt (Mezz) facility to reduce the equity needed to close the transaction.

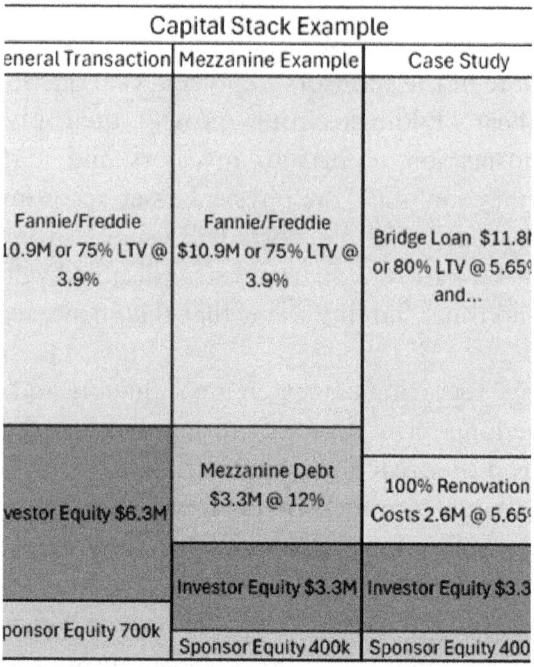

For example, a Mezz facility may take a higher interest rate, 12% but not share in the profits. Some crowdfunding groups treat their investors as a Mezz group and sometimes provide some CoC—usually 6%, paid during the transaction. It's often part of the capital raise, increasing the total project costs. In other structures, the investors may receive an 8% return that may or may not accrue during the transaction horizon in addition to a share of the profits.

Another critical component is the equity invested by the sponsor and the investors. Are the investment amounts treated equally, Pari-Passu, or is there a weighted payout? The equity given by the sponsorship group should be meaningful and exceed their projected transaction fees. Depending on the sponsor's track record, they may invest as little as 5% of the required equity but generally they will provide 20%. In our case study, the sponsor provided 10% of the invested equity.

Next, we need to focus on the projected exit cap, yield to cost, and the market's projected rent growth—generally, a passive investor's control and decision-making end after they have invested. While there are many safeguards within operating agreements to protect an investor, every transaction requires a fine-tooth comb and full underwriting; there are a few metrics we can focus on to save you time and maximize your transaction exposure quickly.

I believe that having a 12-month trailing income and expense statement in addition to the property's Rent Roll cannot be neglected when verifying data. While source data is not critical at this stage, using only the broker-provided Offering Memorandum (OM) or sponsor package may not offer enough or, in some cases, accurate data. Keep in mind that brokers are determined to provide their clients with the best market price. In most cases, a broker is providing the best data they have, but every OM will have a disclaimer: buyer beware.

INCOME & EXPENSE SUMMARY

Income	Current	Per Unit
Gross Potential Rent	$1,248,480	$8,792
Loss to Lease	($92,640)	7.42%
Vacancy Loss	($25,560)	2.05%
Other Rent Loss	($24,970)	2.00%
Total Economic Losses	($143,170)	11.47%
Net Rental Income	**$1,105,310**	**$7,784**
Utility Reimbursement	$0	$0
Other Income	$35,500	$250
Effective Gross Income	**$1,140,810**	**$8,034**

Expenses	Current	Per Unit
Real Estate Taxes	$57,511	$405
Insurance	$35,395	$249
Utilities	$71,038	$500
On-Site Payroll	$122,824	$865
Repairs & Maintenance	$98,417	$500
Contract Services	$25,255	$200
General & Administrative	$12,496	$88
Management Fee	$26,785	$189
Reserves & Replacements	$28,400	$200
Total Expenses	**$478,121**	**$3,367**
Expenses Per Square Foot	$4.63	
% of EGI	43.15%	
Net Operating Income	**$629,930**	**$4,436**

You are solely responsible for independently verifying the information in this Memorandum. ANY RELIANCE ON IT IS SOLELY AT YOUR OWN RISK.

Let us look at an example of a transaction we purchased. You can see that the EGI minus the Total Expenses does not equal the NOI. The actual NOI is $662,689 at a 5% CAP, totaling a value of $13,253,780, vs. the broker-presented NOI of $629,930 at a 5% CAP, totaling a value of $12,598,600. That minor typo has a difference in value of $655,180. Again, note the disclaimer at the bottom of the page.

So, it is always wise to ask for the sponsor's underwriting model. You can determine how the sponsor determines their educated assumptions and how advanced their work is. While all modes and reports adhere to the "garbage in, garbage out" concept, the sophistication level of an underwriting model can help you have insight into business practices and operational acumen.

But there are some sponsors who refuse to send out their models—what can you do about that? Well, it's a red flag for me. It feels like there is something to hide when we are all working off the same numbers and data. So, it is possible that there is a difference in the sponsor's vision, ability to execute, and educated assumptions based on experience.

If you are investing, the sponsor should already have the property under contract. Generally, that means they have been selected from a pool of potential buyers with the highest offer, best terms, and highest certainty of close. However, we have had the highest offer in the past and lost the transaction due to a previous relationship between the chosen buyer and the seller. It isn't always about money.

Once you have the sponsor's model, you should find the rent growth and exit cap rate inputs. If you cannot find the input, consider reviewing the year-over-year (YOY) income and expense increases. I prefer to look at the final year increases. Sometimes, the early years of the sponsor's proforma can include a renovation business plan, loss to lease, or down units polluting the data.

The later years, usually from 5 to 10, should have a standard percentage increase. The increase should range between 2% and 4% depending on the market, job population growth, and economic drivers, but conservatively, it should not exceed 3%. In full disclosure, our case study underwriting had an annual increase of 4%, which we felt was conservative at the time, considering the yearly rental growth was 5% in Phoenix.

The exit CAP should be easy to locate. If not, you can calculate it by dividing the projected sale year NOI by the projected sale price. The industry will generally add 5 to 10 Basis Point Spread (BPS), one-hundredth of one percent (0.01%), per year to the CAP rate. For example, a 5-year horizon can result in an increase of 25 to 50 BPS, a 7-year horizon can increase 35 to 70 BPS, and a 10-year horizon can enhance 50 to 100 BPS. The larger the BPS, the more conservative the underwriting.

The resolution should be an increase above the current market CAP rates. It should offer a buffer for the unexpected, such as COVID, interest rate adjustments, new product absorption, or proposed federal rental increase limits. If you do not know how to find the current market cap rates, I recommend consulting the sponsor, broker, or other credible sources.

Next, we look at operating expenses. If you are exploring a market, you may not be intimately familiar with operating costs, generally calculated per unit per annum (PUPA). Fear not; you can check the historical financial data against the sponsor's projections without knowing specific market or sub-market tendencies. If they are drastically different, ask why.

Listing brokers or sponsors will annualize the previous quarter's (3 months) or the last month's income and compare it with the trailing 12 months of expenses. The expectation is that a property's income should continue to increase monthly, and using the previous quarter can be a good indicator of the property's projected income performance.

A sponsor's proforma usually adjusts their income expectations by verifying the comparable market rents and subtracting loss to lease, vacancy, economic loss, vacancy due to renovation, while adding in, value-add income, other income, and utility reimbursements which will provide you with your EGI. Controllable expenses should change to align with previous sponsorship experience and market data, but they may not necessarily align with the existing trailing expenses. Finally, installing water-reducing devices and LED lighting can reduce utility expenses if managed correctly.

Calculating the asset's Yield to Cost (YTC) will give you a unique metric to compare different properties over time. To calculate Yield to Cost, we divide the final operating year's

NOI by the total project cost. While an IRR can be bent slightly in favor of the sponsor with minor adjustments, the YTC calculation is much more immutable in determining the potential returns.

I hope to help you quickly determine if a multifamily asset is a viable transaction for your investment goals. Underwriting is the first of many steps to purchasing a multifamily asset. We first need to obtain our underwriting materials for the asset you want to consider or, in this case, our case study. Below is the must-have list I look for when underwriting a property for investment or purchase.

- Trailing 12-Month Financial Statement (T12).
- Rent roll (Rent Roll).
- Offering memorandum (Broker OM).
- Underwriting model in Excel.
- Other data sources: CoStar, Yardi Matrix, or National Apartment Association Report.

As a note, an OM can help provide a quick source for unit mix, market data, broker projections, and a prospective business plan but can have inaccurate information. Too often, broker expenses and income projections are aggressive, and to be fair, they are motivated to create the highest and best offer for their client. After extensive repetition of underwriting multiple OMs from different brokers, you can determine, over time, how close their initial marketing packages may align to your underwriting criteria.

You can always source more data to make an educated decision. As you continue to underwrite and gain market experience, more trends and tendencies will reveal themselves. For example, you can source *Yardi Matrix* operating expense information with a simple Google search, giving you a general expense summary of 20,000 current complexes.

Yardi Matrix can be a national average and may not be specific to your market, sponsor expertise, or property nuances.

With quick underwriting and a few data points, we can determine whether to invest with the sponsor group. As a sponsor, submit a Letter of Intent (LOI) with a sensible value or pass on the transaction. For a passive investor or limited partner, a quick and efficient underwriting tool allows you to make educated decisions about your investment.

Most multifamily underwriting models have standard inputs. In most cases, models can include an individual tab for the expected inputs of rent, income, expenses, and year-over-year assumptions. If you are determined to program your model fully, it will formulate the final critical metrics for you. A well-built model will remove many human errors and provide essential information like the purchase cap rate, yield on cost, projected IRR, debt service ratio, and projected annual cash flow.

To wrap up, understanding the concept of apartment sponsorship is vital for anyone looking to dive into the world of multifamily real estate. Sponsorship isn't just about the person or team putting the deal together; it's about the trust and credibility they bring to the table. Sponsors are the linchpin of the investment process, especially when it comes to pooling capital from investors and ensuring the property is managed properly. They serve as the bridge between the investors and the success of the property itself.

Sponsorship also highlights the collaborative nature of real estate investments. A well-executed sponsorship plan can attract investors, secure necessary financing, and foster confidence in all parties involved. Sponsors help shape the direction of the project, providing insight into how the property will be repositioned, managed, and eventually turned into a profit. In essence, an effective sponsor not only brings experience and a track record to the table but also a comprehensive understanding of the complexities involved in apartment investments.

Without a strong sponsor, projects can quickly lose momentum, funding can fall through, and the viability of a property's repositioning can come into question. That's why it's important to vet sponsors with the same intensity that one would vet a property or market. In many ways, a sponsor's reputation and capabilities are directly linked to the success or failure of an investment.

The need for sponsorship in apartment deals becomes particularly evident in larger, more complex projects. Sponsors bring together the right people, capital, and strategies to push a project forward. As an investor or developer, understanding the role of the sponsor gives you a clearer picture of the bigger investment landscape. Now that we've outlined the importance of sponsorship, it's time to dive into the next critical element of apartment investment: underwriting.

While sponsorship provides vision and strategy, underwriting provides the data-driven validation of that vision. It requires an in-depth analysis of the property's financial health, projected returns, and risk factors. The underwriting process essentially answers the question: does this investment make financial sense?

In the following chapter, we'll explore the critical elements of underwriting, the key financial metrics involved, and how investors can assess whether a property is worth the risk.

CHAPTER 2

Underwriting Unlocked

Imagine walking through a construction site. The towering cranes, scaffolding, and raw materials scattered around all hint at the future promise of a completed building. Yet, none of this would exist without a solid blueprint, the silent, guiding document that turns chaos into structure.

In multifamily real estate, underwriting serves as that fundamental blueprint. Without proper underwriting, even the most promising asset can become a liability. This chapter isn't just about crunching numbers—it's about understanding the intricate balance between risk and reward, how small details in financial modeling can shape massive outcomes, and how sound underwriting serves as the foundation for long-term asset management success.

Just as an architect designs with both form and function in mind, your underwriting must account for both the short-term performance and long-term value of your multifamily asset.

In this chapter, we'll break down the key elements of underwriting, highlight common pitfalls to avoid, and walk you through a real-world case study that shows how careful planning today can lead to exceptional returns tomorrow.

First things first, let us understand what underwriting is:

Underwriting is the process of evaluating a multifamily investment's financial viability and potential risks. It involves a detailed analysis of market conditions, financial performance, property operations, and possible future income for multifamily properties. The goal is to determine whether the investment meets the investor's criteria for risk and return.

The importance of underwriting cannot be understated. The objective is to provide a comprehensive analysis for informed investment decisions. Underwriting can identify potential risks and financial vulnerabilities of the asset. It mainly answers the question, "*Is the asset viable to achieve your desired cash flow and returns?*"

Over the following few sections, we will delve into the components of underwriting. Market Analysis will help evaluate market conditions, including rental rates, occupancy levels, job growth, population growth, and economic trends. Financial Analysis will review property income, expenses, and cash flow projections. Deal Structuring will assess financing options, deal structures, and potential tax implications. Risk Assessments will allow us to mitigate potential market, operational, and financial risks.

Underwriting not only assesses financial performance but also identifies areas where operational improvements can create value. For instance, understanding the rent potential in comparison to current lease rates helps pinpoint underutilized income streams. Often, a property's value isn't just in its current state but in its untapped potential; underwriting reveals this potential by evaluating renovation needs, occupancy efficiencies, and ancillary income sources.

Another fundamental part of underwriting is sensitivity analysis. This involves adjusting key variables, like vacancy rates, interest rates, and operating expenses to see how these changes impact overall returns. Sensitivity analysis equips investors with a better understanding of possible outcomes in fluctuating market conditions and aids in decision-making when deciding on investment strategies.

Moreover, the underwriting process typically requires creating a realistic budget for anticipated capital expenditures. These expenditures could include anything from small repairs to substantial renovations. Accurate budgeting for capital improvements is essential for maintaining both the asset's physical condition and its competitive standing in the market.

A thorough underwriting process ensures that you clearly understand the property's financial health and potential and enables you to make informed and strategic investment decisions. The subsequent sections will delve deeper into each aspect of underwriting, providing detailed methodologies and practical insights for conducting effective underwriting for multifamily properties. Below is the sponsor underwriting related to the Case Study.

Sources And Uses Of Funds

Project:
Date: [redacted]

Sources Of Funds			
Bridge Loan			
	Loan Amount:		**$14,200,000**
	Per Unit:	$91,026	
	Per SF:	$135.24	
	Loan To Cost:	79.11%	
Equity			
	LP Equity:	90%	3,374,842
	Sponsor Equity:	10%	374,982
	Total Equity:		**$3,749,825**
			-
Total Project			**$17,949,825**

Entry Cap Rate on Purchase Price	4.61%
Stabilized Debt Yield	8.82%
Exit Capitalization Rate	5.75%
Yield to Cost	7.39%
Developer Spread (Mth 36)	1.64%

Uses Of Funds		
Acquisition Cost:		Per Unit
Purchase Price	14,550,000	93,269
Consulting Fee	218,250	1,399
Closing Cost	36,375	233
Total Acquisition Cost	**14,804,625**	**94,901**
Hard Costs:		
Interior Renovations	1,209,000	7,750
Exterior Renovation	780,000	5,000
Construction Management	198,900	1,275
Hard Cost Contingency	238,680	1,530
Total Hard Costs	**2,426,580**	**15,555**
Soft Costs:		
Architectural, MP&E, Permitting	30,000	192
Legal Fees	125,000	801
Third Party Reports and Survey	50,000	321
Loan Fee	284,000	1,821
Interest Rate Cap	30,000	192
Insurance & Prop Tax Advance	29,620	190
Equity Placement Fee	120,000	769
Total Soft Cost	**668,620**	**4,286**
Operational Reserve	**50,000**	**321**
Total Project	**$17,949,825**	**$115,063**

Decoding Market Dynamics

Understanding the market in which you intend to purchase an asset is the beginning of underwriting a multifamily asset. It offers insights into the local economy, demographic trends, and competitive landscape, all of which influence the property's potential performance. Here's a detailed explanation of the market analysis process:

Economic indicators, such as employment rates, income levels, and economic growth, are fundamental to understanding the health of the local market. A market with high employment rates hints at a stable economy, leading to higher demand for rental properties and potential for rent growth. Understanding the average income levels helps set appropriate rent prices and gauge tenant affordability in conjunction with an immediate area market study. Regions with strong economic and job growth tend to increase property values and rental demand.

As with anything, markets have tiers. For example, P.F. Chang's affiliates with *Pei Wei Asian Diner* and *Panda Express* to cater to a wide range of demographics and clientele. People designate primary, secondary, and tertiary markets with letter grades similar to those used in grade school: A, B, C, and D. When brokers or sponsors want to get creative or need to specify further, they add a plus, minus, or another descriptor.

A primary market is Phoenix, a submarket is Tempe, and an A location is generally lifestyle by choice assets. A secondary market, for example, is Tucson, while a tertiary market would be Sedona. An asset can be in a solid B-plus location, close to a Walmart, on a hard corner with a high traffic count in any of those cities. Still, the rents, expenses, traffic count, job growth, and local ordinances are going to be drastically different.

There is a laundry list of things to consider when entering any market. We seek a thriving local economy with higher-than-average job growth driven by diverse industries. As a rule of thumb, investor groups appreciate the feeling that there is not much market turmoil on the horizon (Holstein, 2020). Transactions are usually ten-year projections and should weather most economic factors or recessions over time. For example, very few groups were prepared for COVID, and I will discuss this topic further in the Operations section of this book.

All states and municipalities approach multifamily differently. While some may favor the landlord, others favor the tenant. Unfortunately, policy is a factor in investment and market analysis. Historically, California, Illinois, and New York have been pro-tenant, while Indiana, Arizona, and Texas favor the landlord (Adam, 2024). The difference between a 5-day notice to vacate and a 30-day notice to vacate is drastic on an operational and economic scale.

Once you have identified the market, you need to examine the area's demographics surrounding the asset. It is vital to understand the age distribution of the surrounding area. Adhering to the Fair Housing Act concerning all things multifamily is mandatory, and it is just as important to know that young professionals, families, and retirees have different housing needs and preferences (Louisiana Realtors, 2022).

The average household size can also influence the demand for different sized units. Some municipalities have a maximum of two people per bedroom, while others subscribe to a "two plus one" rule of two per bedroom and one per living room. The average household size will indicate the need for the unit styles the asset contains.

Areas with high population growth typically experience increased housing demand. Analyzing the current housing supply and demand dynamics can help you understand market saturation. So, evaluate the number of existing rental properties and their occupancy rates. Moreover, consider the impact of new residential properties and assess rental demand through absorption rates. All manner of housing fills this vacuum, including existing single-family homes, new single-family homes, existing rental units, new rental units, build-to-rent single-family homes, manufactured housing, and affordable housing.

A comparative market analysis encompasses studying similar properties to gauge competition and set realistic expectations. The best practice for verifying concessions and renovation nuances is to tour the competition in the market physically. You can compare the rent prices of similar properties to determine competitive pricing for your units.

High occupancy levels in comparable properties can foreshadow strong demand. The generally accepted national average is 95% occupied, 98% often indicating low rents, and 92% being soft, often indicating high rents (Chen, 2020). To be clear, 92% and below can be due to many factors, not just rent pricing, and will be addressed more in the operations section.

Be sure to include the competition's amenities and services in your analysis. Your prospective residents will analyze everything when deciding whether to rent from you or the property down the street, such as:

- *Was the pool clean?*
- *Was the tour path free and clear of trash?*
- *Was the leasing agent engaging and attentive to the prospects' needs?*
- *Was the maintenance staff clean and professional?*
- *Are the blinds in the windows destroyed?*
- *Are patios filled with bikes and debris?*
- *Is the parking lot filled with cars on blocks or potholes?*
- *Were the model lights on?*
- *Were you greeted warmly and with a smile?*

You can leverage various tools and data sources to conduct a thorough market analysis; a subscription may apply. *CoStar* provides commercial real estate market data, including rental and vacancy rates, new developments, ownership, and debt. *Yardi Matrix* offers detailed and real-time information on multifamily properties, occupancy, income and expenses, management, and market trends. The National Apartment Association Report presents industry insights and market trends that can inform your investment decisions. *Apartments.com* can give a general understanding of the rental rates near your Subject Property.

Utilizing these resources can help you gather accurate and up-to-date information to support your market analysis. However, nothing replaces physically touring and driving comparable properties in the Broker OM. Sometimes, the rental rates do not include concessions, which can only be determined by touring or calling the assets.

Also, identify the property's tenant profile. Remembering you are bound by the Fair Housing Act, you need to understand the "typical" resident who lives on the property. Age, income, delinquency, and spatial needs are all part of guaranteeing that there is a demand for your property based on the surrounding market and neighborhood.

The Subject Property of our case study is in a thriving area with strong rental demand, favorable economic indicators, and significant population growth. The demographic analysis showed a diverse tenant base, such as working professionals and families. The competitive landscape was assessed by analyzing nearby properties, rental rates, and occupancy levels. The market analysis suggested a positive outlook for the Subject Property investment, with potential for rent growth and high occupancy rates.

To maximize the potential of your investment, it's essential to approach the market analysis process with both a data-driven strategy and an experiential perspective. By using resources like CoStar and Yardi Matrix, you can collect quantitative data such as rental trends, vacancy rates, and even operational insights into local market dynamics. This information provides a solid foundation for your financial projections and helps in assessing the potential risks and rewards associated with the Subject Property. However, raw data only tells part of the story. For a truly comprehensive perspective, these insights need to be complemented with qualitative observations that come from visiting and evaluating comparable properties firsthand.

Driving through the neighborhood and visiting similar properties will enable you to gauge factors that data alone can't reveal—property maintenance quality, tenant interaction, and neighborhood amenities. Sometimes, advertised rates may exclude concessions or short-term rental incentives, a factor frequently overlooked but impactful on Rent Roll projections. Conversations with on-site leasing staff or tenants can reveal unadvertised concessions, turnover rates, and unique property features that make certain assets more attractive to prospective tenants.

Understanding the tenant profile is another crucial step, particularly in neighborhoods that have experienced recent changes in demographics or property usage. The Fair Housing Act prohibits discriminatory practices, ensuring equal housing opportunities for all. That said, understanding the lifestyle needs and preferences of typical residents—whether they are young professionals seeking proximity to workplaces, families looking for good school districts, or seniors desiring quiet environments—can inform amenity upgrades and marketing approaches that meet the demand without breaching fair housing laws.

In the case of the Subject Property, the positive indicators, such as strong population growth and a diverse demographic profile, reinforce the property's potential for high occupancy and rent appreciation. Nearby employment centers, transportation access, and quality schools are just some of the contributing factors that sustain this demand. Moreover, the demographic insights indicate a balanced tenant mix, which can mean more stable occupancy and lower turnover rates.

Consider the economic growth trajectory of the area as well. Proximity to new job hubs or transit developments, for example, can enhance the desirability of your property. Tracking local employment trends and large-scale projects, such as corporate relocations or public infrastructure improvements, can provide early indicators of rental demand surges. This trend-based approach can enhance your forecasting accuracy and help identify periods when it may be feasible to implement rent increases or restructure lease terms.

Finally, by staying engaged with market reports like those from the National Apartment Association and leveraging listings on platforms like Apartments.com, you can keep a pulse on emerging trends and assess how your property aligns with the local rental ecosystem. This vigilance is key to capitalizing on the property's long-term growth potential, as well as to promptly address any shifts in tenant needs or economic factors that could impact profitability.

Crunching the Numbers

Financial analysis is a pivotal component of underwriting a multifamily asset. It involves evaluating income, expenses, capital expenses, and cash flow projections to determine the potential profitability of the investment. A thorough financial analysis helps anyone understand the property's economic health and make informed decisions.

Understanding financial metrics is essential for evaluating a multifamily investment's potential returns and risks. Here are some of the most discussed metrics:

Net Operating Income (NOI): The total income the property generates after deducting operating expenses but before accounting for debt service and taxes. While it is not the only indicator of the property's financial performance, it is the primary indicator.

Cash-on-Cash (CoC) Return: Divide the annual cash distributed by the total invested capital. Cash-on-

Internal Rate of Return (IRR): The annual growth rate an investment is expected to generate taking into consideration the time value of money and provides a comprehensive view of the investment's profitability.

Cap Rate (CAP): The capitalization rate represents the ratio of NOI to the property's value, indicating the return on investment if purchased entirely with cash and without leveraging debt.

Debt Service Coverage Ratio (DSCR): This ratio measures the property's ability to cover debt obligations by dividing the NOI by the total debt service (principal and interest payments). This calculation can limit the amount of debt a property can support.

Return on Investment (ROI): The initial equity investment return after capital and ownership expenses.

Let us understand this with the help of an example. You can download the case study documents from a QR code later in the book. When underwriting the Subject Property, we based the initial financial projections on detailed market data and the historical performance of similar properties. To accomplish this, we used the Rent Roll (RR) dated February 20, 2019, and the Statement (12 Months) showing monthly financials from February 2018 to January 2019, commonly referred to as a Trailing 12 Months (T12).

Scheduled Rental Income on this T12 comprises Gross Potential Rent (GPR) and Loss/Gain to Lease (LTL). The GPR should match the expected market rent of all your units. Gross Potential Rent represents the maximum amount your asset could collect if all units were rented at market rates. It is interesting as this subject property fluctuates each month. As a general rule, the GPR should continue to increase due to repositioning renovations, inflation, market supply and demand, and population supply and demand.

Period = Feb 2018-Jan 2019

Book = Accrual ; Tree = ysi_is

		Feb 2018	Mar 2018	Apr 2018	May 2018	Jun 2018	Jul 2018	Aug 2018	Sep 2018	Oct 2018	Nov 2018	Dec 2018	Jan 2019	Total
4000-0000	**INCOME**													
4100-0000	RENT INCOME													
4300-0000	Gross Potential Rent	117,065.00	115,725.00	122,450.00	133,365.00	127,750.00	122,940.00	118,735.00	122,535.00	128,900.00	119,940.00	123,105.00	128,395.00	1,480,905.00
4400-0000	Loss/Gain to Lease	-9,847.00	-7,670.00	-11,729.00	-23,137.00	-16,125.00	-10,686.00	-6,587.00	-10,453.00	-16,309.00	-7,142.00	-10,171.00	-15,289.00	-145,145.00
4590-0000	TOTAL SCHEDULED RENT	107,218.00	108,055.00	110,721.00	110,228.00	111,625.00	112,254.00	112,148.00	112,082.00	112,591.00	112,798.00	112,934.00	113,106.00	1,335,760.00
4700-0000	RENT LOSS													
4710-0000	Less: Concessions	-175.00	-163.71	-161.67	-147.58	-150.00	-936.29	-1,525.00	-1,325.00	-75.75	-75.00	-75.00	-75.00	-4,885.00
4730-0000	Less: Vacancy	-3,306.27	-5,500.69	-7,324.42	-4,176.28	-6,101.96	-9,069.70	-8,049.92	-5,731.25	-6,396.14	-5,775.61	-4,029.06	-4,233.56	-69,694.86
4735-0000	Less: Employee Apartments	-1,183.22	-994.11	-994.11	-994.11	-994.11	-994.11	-994.11	-994.11	-189.11	-189.11	-189.11	-189.11	-8,898.43
4740-0000	Less: Model Apartments	-710.00	-680.00	0.00	0.00	0.00	0.00	0.00	0.00	0.00	0.00	-720.00	-710.00	-2,820.00
4750-0000	Less: Rent Write Off	-14.03	-435.09	-713.64	0.00	0.00	-270.53	-665.88	-12.43	0.00	-56.68	-527.33	40.32	-2,655.29
4890-0000	TOTAL RENT LOSS	-5,388.52	-7,773.60	-9,193.84	-5,317.97	-7,246.07	-11,270.63	-11,234.91	-8,062.79	-6,661.00	-6,096.40	-5,540.50	-5,167.35	-88,953.58
4990-0000	NET RENTAL INCOME	101,829.48	100,281.40	101,527.16	104,910.03	104,378.93	100,983.37	100,913.09	104,019.21	105,930.00	106,701.60	107,393.50	107,938.65	1,246,806.42
5600-0000	OTHER RENTAL INCOME													
5605-0000	Application Fees	280.00	910.00	735.00	350.00	700.00	560.00	840.00	700.00	665.00	490.00	315.00	595.00	7,140.00
5606-0000	Cleaning Fees	620.00	725.00	420.00	830.00	680.00	825.00	650.00	410.00	1,065.00	250.00	165.00	401.42	7,041.42
5607-0000	Rent-MTM Fee	192.86	100.00	200.00	100.00	173.26	336.53	258.06	449.95	3.00	0.00	0.00	0.00	1,813.66
5608-0000	Pet Rent	325.00	301.61	325.00	308.87	236.67	187.10	150.00	150.00	150.00	169.17	170.16	157.26	2,630.84
5609-0000	Convenience Fees	85.00	110.00	120.00	125.00	130.00	115.00	165.00	75.00	160.00	400.00	30.00	165.00	1,680.00
5615-0000	Lease Break Fee	3,398.00	4,246.00	4,269.00	1,470.00	2,660.00	2,870.00	3,080.00	0.00	4,444.00	0.00	1,552.00	1,290.00	29,279.00
5625-0000	Damages	760.00	895.00	755.00	845.00	800.00	965.00	787.50	440.00	1,400.00	125.00	245.00	1,059.00	9,076.50
5630-0000	Non Refundable Fees	300.00	150.00	0.01	0.00	0.00	150.00	0.00	0.00	0.00	150.00	150.00	150.00	1,050.01
5663-0000	Bad Debt Expense	-3,319.41	-5,508.62	-7,364.91	-5,422.16	-2,565.64	-6,438.17	-6,132.07	-244.92	-4,254.71	-3,602.00	-2,271.79	-40.32	-47,164.72
5710-0000	Vending Machine Income	0.00	0.00	0.00	0.00	274.47	0.00	0.00	0.00	0.00	0.00	0.00	0.00	274.47
5715-0000	Cable Income	545.52	0.00	0.00	697.54	0.00	0.00	750.84	0.00	0.00	647.23	0.00	0.00	2,641.13
5720-0000	Interest Income	0.00	0.00	0.00	0.00	0.00	0.00	0.00	0.00	0.00	0.00	38.86	0.00	38.86
5800-0000	Late Fee	1,145.00	1,395.00	1,100.74	1,635.00	1,810.00	2,480.00	2,095.00	2,490.00	2,540.00	1,910.00	1,605.00	2,755.00	22,960.74
5807-0000	Legal Fees	773.00	771.00	573.00	401.00	585.00	385.00	816.00	733.00	245.00	210.00	70.00	715.00	6,277.00
5808-0000	Admin Fees	0.00	500.00	397.74	597.75	497.75	597.56	700.00	900.00	995.50	595.32	500.00	500.00	6,781.62
5810-0000	NSF Fees	50.00	50.00	0.00	0.00	50.00	50.00	50.00	0.00	50.00	50.00	0.00	50.00	400.00
5814-0000	Renters Insurance	1,462.67	1,459.77	1,464.29	1,495.07	1,475.28	1,436.01	1,448.57	1,458.31	1,494.43	1,508.59	1,538.15	1,533.99	17,775.13
5820-0000	RUBS	5,756.45	5,614.18	5,519.42	5,592.85	5,893.28	5,675.07	5,867.83	6,091.92	6,893.15	6,976.97	6,599.56	7,470.42	73,951.10
5890-0000	TOTAL OTHER RENTAL INCOME	12,374.09	11,718.94	8,514.29	9,025.92	13,400.07	10,194.10	11,526.73	13,653.26	15,850.37	9,880.28	10,706.94	16,801.77	143,646.76

[redacted]

Statement (12 months)

Period = Feb 2018-Jan 2019

Book = Accrual ; Tree = ysi_is

		Feb 2018	Mar 2018	Apr 2018	May 2018	Jun 2018	Jul 2018	Aug 2018	Sep 2018	Oct 2018	Nov 2018	Dec 2018	Jan 2019	Total
6560-0000	Electricity-House Accts	1,346.97	1,424.30	1,318.23	1,449.55	1,306.97	1,669.45	1,039.95	1,543.06	1,509.71	1,400.55	1,488.59	1,454.96	16,952.29
6561-0000	Electricity-Vacant Units	166.05	45.62	636.16	667.11	409.93	394.32	1,053.42	300.55	242.79	237.68	447.73	0.00	4,601.36
6563-0000	Water & Sewer	8,862.36	8,337.18	10,058.84	9,542.54	10,841.94	11,175.38	9,645.33	10,747.25	7,899.65	8,772.36	8,570.70	7,176.66	111,630.19
6564-0000	Trash Disposal	1,000.80	1,735.16	1,083.92	1,776.72	308.00	1,042.36	1,042.36	1,043.00	1,041.72	1,042.36	616.00	1,042.36	12,774.76
6590-0000	TOTAL UTILITIES	11,376.18	11,542.26	13,097.15	13,435.92	12,866.84	14,281.51	12,781.06	13,633.86	10,693.87	11,452.95	11,123.02	9,673.98	145,958.60
6600-0000	MARKETING & RETENTION EXPS													
6602-0000	Internet-Online Advertising	1,637.47	1,843.17	2,226.94	1,587.93	1,527.93	2,067.86	907.68	907.68	2,334.28	1,570.71	2,204.60	1,766.80	20,583.05
6603-0000	Promotions	0.00	0.00	0.00	119.03	0.00	0.00	0.00	0.00	0.00	0.00	0.00	0.00	119.03
6604-0000	Community Events	0.00	350.00	0.00	0.00	350.00	0.00	0.00	350.00	0.00	0.00	350.00	0.00	1,400.00
6606-0000	Hospitality	66.60	5.97	0.00	139.05	52.61	103.00	347.21	-27.95	96.75	79.58	140.24	75.06	1,078.12
6608-0000	Printing	0.00	186.96	4.29	0.00	0.00	0.00	94.82	0.00	79.64	451.93	0.00	0.00	817.64
6615-0000	Property Signage	0.00	-677.23	218.10	49.18	629.20	30.94	0.00	65.66	0.00	0.00	0.00	846.09	1,161.94
6690-0000	TOTAL MARKETING & RETENTION EXPENSES	1,704.07	1,708.87	2,449.33	1,895.19	2,559.74	2,201.80	1,349.71	1,295.39	2,510.67	2,102.22	2,694.84	2,687.95	25,159.78
6699-0000	PAYROLL & BENEFIT EXPENSES													
6700-0000	Salary - Community Manager	3,296.00	4,944.00	3,296.00	3,296.00	3,296.00	3,296.00	3,501.51	3,296.00	3,296.00	3,296.00	3,296.00	3,328.80	41,438.31
6705-0000	Bonus - Community Manager	937.00	1,250.00	625.00	1,250.00	580.85	937.00	1,127.83	625.00	937.00	937.00	625.00	1,250.00	11,081.68
6712-0000	Salary - Asst Manager	769.59	647.05	642.19	464.89	412.28	283.81	592.01	390.84	574.52	324.66	0.00	0.00	5,101.84
6716-0000	Salary - Leasing	2,728.68	2,963.45	1,910.37	1,892.64	1,878.00	1,896.36	2,021.10	1,122.53	2,290.21	2,121.94	2,182.96	2,125.58	25,133.82
6717-0000	Leasing - Renewal Incentives	1,082.66	910.31	939.60	1,792.80	1,362.52	1,271.30	5,611.63	2,396.98	1,957.96	1,969.30	1,446.63	875.20	21,616.89
6718-0000	Salary - Maint Supervisor	3,463.90	5,388.13	3,601.78	3,438.89	3,494.15	3,754.84	4,492.82	3,851.81	3,790.83	3,557.26	3,661.53	3,640.46	46,136.40
6719-0000	Bonus - Maint Supervisor	102.40	546.00	273.00	546.00	273.00	410.00	1,344.31	273.00	410.00	273.00	273.00	546.00	5,269.71
6725-0000	Salary - Maint Technician	2,405.60	3,846.92	2,502.60	2,604.18	2,458.40	2,474.11	2,807.72	3,394.54	896.00	2,659.60	2,624.08	2,606.02	31,279.77
6730-0000	Salary - Turn Crew	2,335.01	896.52	77.63	574.20	87.93	334.29	84.14	0.00	1,566.76	543.40	0.00	0.00	6,499.88
6740-0000	Temp Help - Administrative	0.00	0.00	0.00	0.00	0.00	0.00	0.00	1,740.18	1,126.34	0.00	0.00	1,012.00	3,878.52
6742-0000	Temp Help - Maintenance	0.00	0.00	0.00	0.00	0.00	0.00	0.00	0.00	916.08	0.00	0.00	0.00	916.08
6750-0000	Payroll Taxes	1,556.72	1,730.20	1,048.14	1,517.30	1,259.21	1,376.20	1,781.54	1,311.46	1,377.00	1,403.21	1,174.51	1,861.59	17,397.08
6755-0000	Workers Compensation-Properties	200.11	250.03	162.09	185.37	359.98	399.83	561.80	424.01	385.99	398.03	369.83	370.56	4,067.63
6775-0000	Insurance - Medical & Other Benefits	1,447.13	1,395.48	1,395.44	1,465.78	719.54	1,461.09	2,040.76	946.31	900.60	1,079.41	1,352.38	1,253.74	15,457.66
6800-0000	Payroll Fees	566.93	533.49	276.68	689.87	799.40	853.49	1,021.21	616.86	737.72	772.04	762.44	762.44	8,392.57
6990-0000	TOTAL PAYROLL EXPENSES	20,891.73	25,301.58	16,750.52	19,717.92	16,981.26	18,748.32	26,988.38	20,389.52	21,163.01	19,334.85	17,768.36	19,632.39	243,667.84
7000-0000	GENERAL & ADMINISTRATIVE													
7112-0000	Hiring Costs	64.87	98.95	23.30	5.01	0.00	197.44	32.24	55.45	113.75	0.00	0.00	0.00	591.01
7115-0000	Advertising & Marketing	0.00	81.50	58.51	97.26	0.00	159.28	0.00	0.00	368.97	0.00	-349.00	0.00	416.52
7135-0000	Auto & Parking Expense	20.33	47.93	48.79	34.56	40.26	25.68	48.04	34.67	15.73	73.62	81.82	12.84	484.27
7145-0000	Bank Fees	139.29	144.42	133.70	223.63	100.34	118.68	76.72	130.60	70.56	77.73	99.72	47.20	1,362.59
7150-0000	Internet/Cable Service	206.99	206.99	413.98	206.99	206.99	206.99	206.99	206.99	206.99	0.00	590.67	407.24	3,067.81
7175-0000	Computer Expense-Consultants	0.00	84.76	34.32	0.00	318.38	15.18	72.65	0.00	0.00	0.00	120.00	0.00	645.29
7180-0000	Computer Expense-Email Hosting	152.43	0.00	0.00	0.00	0.00	0.00	0.00	0.00	0.00	0.00	0.00	0.00	152.43

[redacted]

Statement (12 months)

Period = Feb 2018-Jan 2019

Book = Accrual ; Tree = ysi_is

		Feb 2018	Mar 2018	Apr 2018	May 2018	Jun 2018	Jul 2018	Aug 2018	Sep 2018	Oct 2018	Nov 2018	Dec 2018	Jan 2019	Total
7181-0000	Computer Equipment	80.56	0.00	0.00	0.00	0.00	0.00	0.00	0.00	0.00	0.00	0.00	0.00	80.56
7185-0000	Computer & Internet-Software & Fees	0.00	0.00	0.00	0.00	49.85	0.00	0.00	0.00	0.00	0.00	0.00	0.00	49.85
7186-0000	Convention & Seminar Fees	0.00	0.00	0.00	0.00	24.17	0.00	0.00	0.00	0.00	0.00	0.00	0.00	24.17
7187-0000	Credit Check/Screening	135.28	173.94	483.16	405.85	173.94	419.94	342.64	464.00	381.01	320.17	687.37	207.35	4,194.65
7188-0000	Credit Card Processing Fees	277.98	290.63	398.98	347.45	390.16	335.78	312.34	352.17	298.67	152.92	97.65	155.66	3,410.39
7202-0000	Dues & Subscriptions	1,046.77	1,646.59	1,650.34	2,273.34	1,264.66	1,907.79	1,708.24	1,339.52	1,907.45	1,455.36	1,878.73	1,264.45	19,343.24
7203-0000	Renter's Legal Liability	1,232.25	1,264.05	1,232.25	1,232.25	1,232.25	1,232.25	1,232.25	1,240.20	1,248.15	1,232.25	1,232.50	1,232.00	14,842.65
7215-0000	Entertainment & Business Meals	21.99	0.00	0.00	66.94	0.00	0.00	79.52	0.00	43.43	46.40	609.81	41.45	909.54
7216-0000	Shopping Reports	350.00	0.00	350.00	0.00	0.00	0.00	0.00	0.00	0.00	0.00	350.00	0.00	1,050.00
7217-0000	Employee Training	0.00	53.04	594.07	53.04	-27.11	53.04	53.04	63.67	106.08	53.04	53.04	83.68	1,138.63
7218-0000	Team Building Events	0.00	715.16	7.26	0.00	0.00	0.00	0.00	0.00	0.00	0.00	0.00	86.66	809.08
7220-0000	Equipment Rental	17.21	202.07	104.68	103.05	84.98	117.65	116.08	145.38	91.58	115.77	112.97	103.04	1,314.46
7222-0000	Uniforms	22.49	52.01	9.66	578.89	99.67	128.52	0.00	374.50	0.00	0.00	0.00	0.00	1,265.74
7290-0000	Legal Fees-Eviction Fees	302.00	662.00	708.00	33.00	188.00	625.00	10.46	925.54	0.00	150.00	590.00	561.00	4,755.00
7300-0000	Postage	8.15	14.19	0.00	0.00	0.00	0.00	30.76	0.00	0.00	0.00	0.00	0.00	53.10
7305-0000	Professional Fees	0.00	0.00	0.00	0.00	0.00	0.00	0.00	0.00	1,236.68	0.00	0.00	0.00	1,236.68
7415-0000	Telephone Expense	343.19	323.19	420.42	277.82	342.82	329.65	277.17	696.42	342.91	200.59	540.85	290.80	4,385.83
7420-0000	Office Supplies	114.10	110.95	0.00	114.97	153.45	151.34	117.64	88.33	243.76	123.54	71.47	222.56	1,512.11
7620-0000	Taxes & Licenses	0.00	0.00	270.00	0.00	0.00	21.96	0.00	0.00	0.00	0.00	50.00	0.00	341.96
7790-0000	TOTAL G & A EXPENSES	4,535.88	6,172.37	6,941.42	6,054.05	4,642.81	6,046.17	4,716.78	6,117.44	6,675.72	4,001.39	6,817.60	4,715.93	67,437.56
7791-0000	PROPERTY MANAGEMENT FEES													
7795-0000	Property Management Fees	3,481.97	3,335.65	3,340.34	3,404.60	3,480.32	3,534.53	3,389.25	3,364.52	3,471.32	3,617.75	3,563.53	3,580.27	41,564.05
7799-0000	TOTAL PROPERTY MANAGEMENT FEES	3,481.97	3,335.65	3,340.34	3,404.60	3,480.32	3,534.53	3,389.25	3,364.52	3,471.32	3,617.75	3,563.53	3,580.27	41,564.05
7990-0000	TOTAL CONTROLLABLE EXPENSES	49,199.46	54,064.12	48,799.46	53,495.50	49,034.60	53,579.12	58,106.56	53,010.07	53,858.42	48,301.99	49,264.92	44,940.29	615,654.51
7992-0000	*NET INCOME/(LOSS) AFTER CONTROLLABLE EXPENS*	*65,004.11*	*57,936.22*	*61,241.99*	*60,440.45*	*68,744.40*	*57,598.35*	*54,333.26*	*64,662.40*	*67,921.95*	*68,279.89*	*68,835.52*	*79,800.13*	*774,798.67*
7993-0000	PROPERTY TAXES													
7995-0000	Real Estate Tax	7,512.34	7,512.34	7,512.34	7,512.34	7,512.34	7,512.34	7,512.34	7,512.34	7,512.34	7,838.20	7,541.96	7,512.34	90,503.56
7996-0000	TOTAL PROPERTY TAXES	7,512.34	7,512.34	7,512.34	7,512.34	7,512.34	7,512.34	7,512.34	7,512.34	7,512.34	7,838.20	7,541.96	7,512.34	90,503.56
7997-0000	PROPERTY INSURANCE													
7998-0000	Property & Liability Insurance	1,862.00	1,862.00	1,862.00	1,862.00	1,862.00	1,862.00	1,862.00	1,862.00	1,862.00	1,862.00	0.00	3,713.00	22,333.00
7999-0000	TOTAL PROPERTY INSURANCE	1,862.00	1,862.00	1,862.00	1,862.00	1,862.00	1,862.00	1,862.00	1,862.00	1,862.00	1,862.00	0.00	3,713.00	22,333.00
7999-0999	TOTAL NONCONTROLLABLE EXPENSES	9,374.34	9,374.34	9,374.34	9,374.34	9,374.34	9,374.34	9,374.34	9,374.34	9,374.34	9,700.20	7,541.96	11,225.34	112,836.56

Some companies use a Lease Rent Optimization (LRO) system that adjusts the market rent daily based on the availability of each unit style. For example, if five one-bedroom units are available on Monday, the software prices them at $700. If two of these units quickly rent out because the competition is priced at $775, the software raises the price to $765 on Tuesday morning. After your all-star leasing staff rents two more units, the software sets the cost of the last remaining unit at $900 on Wednesday morning due to its limited availability.

Aside from the fact that your staff must take time every morning to determine the price and reference a pricing sheet while talking to a prospect, causing awkward silences and the appearance of a lack of knowledge, the unit may sit vacant for the rest of the month, losing $900 because the software couldn't self-correct. Management should fix this extreme example with rental limits and parameters, but it can often be overlooked or take days to resolve. Why am I telling you all of this in detail? I explain all this to emphasize that the GPR can fluctuate month by month without logic in an LRO-based property.

The LTL is the difference between the property market rent and the leased rent. The lease rent can be lower for multiple reasons, including a previously provided reoccurring concession. A recurring concession is a big no-no in this industry, as shown in unit 167 of the RR. Financially, you are better off providing a one-time concession instead of spreading it over multiple months.

Most of the time, a long-term resident experiences minor rent increases over the years compared to the market rate for new move-ins. Unit 110, a one-bedroom, one-bathroom apartment rented on January 15, 2012, is currently charged $516 for rent plus $9.95 for renters insurance, while the market rent for that apartment is $915. By subtracting the market rent of $915 and the current leased rent of $516, the result is a $399 loss to lease (LTL).

Rent Rolls have individual codes and billing line items for each resident, which can include everything from the typical pet rent, renters insurance, cable and internet, Resident Utility Billing System (RUBS), and parking to the more obscure amenity rent, carport rent, rubbish valet, package service, dry cleaning service, and on and on.

The rental income is conveniently summarized at the bottom of the RR. The monthly rent is $112k, while the T12 shows $113k billed in January. That can differ due to partial month move-in prorations or other back-end accounting items, but it shouldn't be off by much. Adjusting for concessions, vacancy, employee apartment credits, model apartments, and rent write-offs.

Below, you will find an example of a Rent Roll with Lease Charges containing multiple references including a middle and the last page of the Rent Roll to demonstrate the mentioned difference.

Rent Roll with Lease Charges

[redacted]

As Of = 02/20/2019

Month Year = 02/2019

Unit	Unit Type	Unit Sq Ft	Resident	Name	Market Charge	Rent Code	Amount	Resident Deposit	Other Deposit	Move In	Lease Expiration	Move Out	Balance
145	k2x1	750.00	[redacted]	[redacted] [redacted]	905.00	rent	805.00	0.00	0.00	09/01/2018	10/31/2019		-310.00
						rll	10.95						
						Total	**815.95**						
146	k1x1	600.00	[redacted]	[redacted]	915.00	rent	627.00	250.00	0.00	12/08/2011	05/31/2019		0.00
						rll	9.95						
						Total	**636.95**						
147	k1x1	600.00	[redacted]	[redacted]	915.00	rent	615.00	250.00	0.00	08/02/2014	08/31/2019		0.00
						rll	9.95						
						Total	**624.95**						
148	k2x1	750.00	[redacted]	[redacted]	905.00	rent	776.00	250.00	0.00	09/17/2016	07/16/2019		-12.19
						rll	9.95						
						Total	**785.95**						
149	k2x1	750.00	[redacted]	[redacted]	905.00	rent	798.00	249.00	0.00	07/10/2017	07/09/2019		0.00
						petrent	25.00						
						rll	9.95						
						Total	**832.95**						
150	k1x1	600.00	[redacted]	[redacted]	915.00	rent	715.00	715.00	0.00	07/23/2018	03/22/2019		0.00
						rll	9.95						
						Total	**724.95**						
151	k1x1	600.00	[redacted]	[redacted]	780.00	rent	675.00	0.00	0.00	10/04/2018	07/03/2019	03/13/2019	-0.27
						rll	10.95						
						Total	**685.95**						
152	k2x1	750.00	[redacted]	[redacted]	880.00	rent	810.00	810.00	0.00	09/29/2018	08/30/2019		-26.19
						rll	10.95						
						Total	**820.95**						
153	k2x1	750.00	[redacted]	[redacted]	900.00	rent	820.00	805.00	0.00	03/19/2018	05/18/2019		0.00
						rll	9.95						
						Total	**829.95**						
154	k1x1	600.00	[redacted]	[redacted]	915.00	rent	715.00	715.00	0.00	08/24/2018	10/23/2019		-0.11
						rll	10.95						
						Total	**725.95**						
155	k1x1	600.00	[redacted]	[redacted]	915.00	rent	675.00	675.00	0.00	08/31/2018	10/30/2019		-0.59
						rll	10.95						

Rent Roll with Lease Charges

[redacted]

As Of = 02/20/2019

Month Year = 02/2019

Unit	Unit Type	Unit Sq Ft	Resident	Name	Market Rent	Charge Code	Amount	Resident Deposit	Other Deposit	Move In	Lease Expiration	Move Out	Balance
						rfl	10.95						
						Total	**710.95**						
278	k1x1	600.00	[redacted]	[redacted]	895.00	rent	695.00	695.00	0.00	05/04/2018	05/03/2019		0.00
						rfl	9.95						
						rentcdt	-25.00						
						Total	**679.95**						
Future Residents/Applicants													
139	k1x1	600.00	[redacted]	[redacted]	915.00		0.00	0.00	0.00	03/08/2019	05/07/2020		71.61
						Total	**0.00**						
226	k1x1	600.00	[redacted]	[redacted]	895.00		0.00	0.00	0.00	02/22/2019	04/21/2020		35.81
						Total	**0.00**						
		Total		[redacted]	**140,085.00**		**114,502.35**	**70,872.00**	**0.00**				**1,948.91**

Summary Groups	Square Footage	Market Rent	Lease Charges	Security Deposit	Other Deposits	# Of Units	% Unit Occupancy	% Sqft Occupied	Balance
Current/Notice/Vacant Residents	105,000.00	140,085.00	114,502.35	70,872.00	0.00	156.00	98.71	98.85	1,841.49
Future Residents/Applicants	1,200.00	1,810.00	0.00	0.00	0.00	2.00			107.42
Occupied Units	103,800.00	138,275.00				154	98.71	98.85	
Total Non Rev Units	600.00	915.00				1	0.64	0.57	
Total Vacant Units	600.00	895.00				1	0.64	0.57	
Totals:	**105,000.00**	**140,085.00**	**114,502.35**	**70,872.00**	**0.00**	**156**	**100.00**	**100.00**	**1,948.91**

Summary of Charges by Charge Code (Current/Notice Residents Only)

Charge Code	Amount
rent	112,567.00
rfl	1,590.35
rentcdt	-75.00
petrent	225.00
rubs	95.00
mtm	100.00
Total	**114,502.35**

Moving to the Other Rental Income, which includes ancillary income sources, such as laundry facilities, parking, and pet fees, the 12-month statement shows $143k over the previous 12 months. In this case, the management company has also placed the bad debt expense in this category. I have seen this line item also listed in Rent Loss and, if you can believe it, under the General and Administrative section of a T12 (Trailing 12 months definition and explanation, 2022). A reminder: in most cases, a T12 and RR only indicate what has been billed, not what has been collected. The only balance indicator is the far-right column of the RR showing any balances for residents.

A bad debt expense occurs when a resident moves out with a past-due balance and/or physical damages to the unit beyond normal wear and tear, exceeding the security deposit. We will see much of this through the case study due to COVID. All unpaid rent was eventually eliminated in this line and rarely collected.

Generally, when a property writes off the bad debt expense, the debt is sent to a third-party collection company, hoping for a 10% recapture rate and praying for 30%. This is cash that never gets collected, and during COVID, this line item climbed to over 20% in some of our assets. *I never thought I would have to decide between retaining excellent staff or replacing a chiller* and *boiler system, because so many people stopped paying rent.*

Expenses involve many categories, maintenance expenses, turnover expenses, utilities, marketing and retention, payroll and benefits expenses, general and administrative, and property management fees. Those are often referred to as controllable expenses because the management company controls those line items. On the other hand, property taxes and insurance are considered uncontrollable expenses because the municipality sets the tax requirements, and the insurance companies charge whatever the market can stand, which is eventually passed onto the resident as a rental increase.

The income and expenses thus far provide only part of the picture. The NOI will allow you to determine the property's worth, how much debt it can support, and, eventually, how much cash flow will exist.

Below the debt and ownership expenses lay the Capital Expenditures (CapX). Lenders require a minimum reserve to be sent in monthly, ranging from $250 PUPA to above $500 PUPA as part of the lending agreement. Generally, the newer the property, the lower the requirement. These funds can be drawn quarterly or semi-annually for new appliances, carpets, cabinets, water heaters, air conditioners, or roof replacements. However, you will find that even with best practices, the most well-maintained assets average $400 PUPA to appropriately schedule long-term capital improvements.

During the underwriting process, in some cases, you can receive the capital expenses information, allowing you to see what additional costs have been incurred for appliances, windows, flooring, water damage, mold remediation, or other significant capital repairs. This T12 does not have those expenses listed. You can request additional explanations and extensive historical documents during the Due Diligence (DD) process.

Structuring for Success

The next step in the underwriting process is deciding how you will structure your transaction. It determines how the acquisition of a multifamily property will be financed and managed, and this is just the tip of the iceberg. Effective deal structuring makes sure that the investment is financially viable and aligns with the investors' strategic goals. It can also define your investor pool if you are a syndicator.

We will focus on the primary aspects of deal structuring: the financing options available to multifamily transactions, the equity and debt ratio, some negotiable terms in the financing world, and the verbiage associated. Your individual needs and the chosen financing facility can adjust the structure for every transaction, so your sponsor must have a vision for the project.

Evaluating various financing options throughout your underwriting process allows your investors to secure the best terms and maximize returns. There are multiple options, including both recourse and nonrecourse. In a recourse loan, the borrower is personally liable for the debt, providing the lender access to other personal assets to recover in the case of a default. On the other hand, a non-recourse loan limits the lender's recovery to the specified collateral in the loan agreement, typically the property itself.

Four significant categories exist when discussing financing options for your deal structuring:

- Traditional mortgages
- Private equity
- Government-backed loans
- Bridge loans

Traditional mortgages that a local or regional bank provides are usually the most flexible in terms and conditions. Each bank has different criteria and spreads, but most banks will require that you place funds on deposit or hold your operating accounts at their branches for additional favorable terms. Banks can lend at 10x their deposits on hand with limited risk, so by bringing in your business, generally, they can lend more to others than they have lent to you based on your new deposits. These mortgages can be very relationship-based.

Private equity can include capital from private investors or firms. It can also include family offices, life insurance companies, pension funds, or people who want to invest in multifamily assets as debt facilities. In some cases, they can be looking for a portion of the equity and offer additional and significant capital for acquisitions with that as a trade-off. The criteria required here can also be relationship-based but can have stringent criteria.

The most common debt facility in the multifamily space is the United States government. Government-backed loans are guaranteed by agencies, like Fannie Mae, Freddie Mac, or the Department of Housing and Urban Development (HUD). These loans, often non-recourse, come with favorable terms, lower interest rates, longer repayment periods, and interest-only (IO) periods. HUD, in particular, can provide favorable rates and repayment terms of up to 40 years but can take up to 1 year to fund, causing interest rate risk. Fannie Mae and Freddie Mac on the other hand can fund in 30 to 90 days, depending on the transaction, sponsor, and if it is a refinance or acquisition.

These government-backed loans have occupancy benchmarks of 90% over the previous 90 days before funding, causing coordination with current ownership and a risk to any new buyer if it is time to close and the asset is at 89% on the Rent Roll. Sometimes, Rent Rolls do not match the physical occupancy, which we will get into more during the due diligence section.

Bridge loans offer a short-term financing solution for properties that require extensive renovation or stabilization due to mismanagement or cannot meet the 90% occupancy for 90 consecutive days. These loans typically finance the property during these transitional periods, giving the necessary capital until long-term financing can be secured. Bridge loans can give high leverage and renovation funding, usually at a higher interest rate than the previous options.

Analyzing the equity ratio needed to invest in multiple debt facilities can take some time. Still, the right balance can significantly impact the investment opportunity's potential returns and overall risk. Using higher levels of debt or leverage can amplify returns on equity just as it allows investors to control more significant assets with a smaller initial investment. Increased leverage also increases risk; the obligation to make debt payments remains regardless of the property's performance or other external factors (COVID). Relying more heavily on equity reduces the financial risk but can dilute ownership and potentially lower the return on the investment. Finding the right balance is influenced by various factors, including market conditions, investor risk tolerance, and the specific goal of the investment.

As you navigate the different debt facilities, each condition and term is up for negotiation. The answer is no unless you ask; sometimes, it is worth asking. The primary items that can be discussed are whether the interest rates are fixed or variable, the Loan-to-Value ratio (LTV), the Loan-to-Cost ratio (LTC), the repayment schedule, the Debt Service Coverage ratio (DSCR), and, if you are fortunate or are a returning client, the covenants.

The LTV is specific to the existing value of the proposed property, which is verified by a third-party appraisal team hired by the lender. At the same time, the LTC can also include any renovation budget, additional fees, or capital expenses.

HUD, Fannie, and Freddie all focus on the LTV of the asset as it exists, requiring anyone looking to renovate the asset to raise additional capital to fund the repositioning. A short-term bridge facility that is market-dependent will also lend to the seasoned borrower a percentage of the renovation costs, requiring less equity and increasing returns. The drastically glaring risk is that the borrower is asking for more money than the property is worth or can support in the current state.

Each debt facility will focus on different negotiable terms. HUD will generally lend to an x1.175 DSCR, while Fannie and Freddie will only lend to x1.25-x1.35 DSCR. That can mean that your property is debt-constrained due to income. DSCR can limit borrowing to less than the maximum LTV or LTC percentages generally offered. Another factor that can alter the DSCR is the amortization of the payment schedule. HUD offers 40-year amortization while Fannie and Freddie provide 30-year amortization; when you stretch the facility over an additional 10 years, the payments go down, adjusting the DSCR calculation (Iancu, 2024).

Once you have determined the general debt facility you intend to pursue based on your business plan, interest rates, funding estimations, and investor returns, you must mentally process the investment entity structure most viable to manage the property and protect the investors' interests. Common structures include Limited Liability Companies (LLC), Real Estate Investment Trust (REIT), Partnerships, Tenants in Common (TIC), or a combination of these, solely dependent on your investor's long-term criteria.

By spending the time early on to structure the transaction effectively, investors can optimize returns, manage risks, and confirm the financial viability of the investment. The Subject Property highlights the importance of a thorough and strategic approach to deal structuring, demonstrating how careful planning and negotiation can lead to a successful investment outcome.

Balance Risk and Reward

Risk assessment, fondly referred to as stress testing, is the final component of underwriting a multifamily property. It entails identifying potential risks, analyzing their impact, and cultivating mitigation strategies. A thorough risk assessment ensures that the sponsors know the challenges they might face and can take proactive measures to protect the investments.

In any multifamily transaction, there are internal and external risks, as well as controllable and uncontrollable risks. A good sponsor does all it can to mitigate those risks, and in transparency, those risks are usually stumbling blocks that cost time and money when you encounter them the first time. The due diligence section of the book will expand on this. The risks that come to mind from an overarching perspective include market adjustment, operational, financial, regulatory, environmental, and tenant.

Financial risks are another critical area to consider, as they encompass fluctuations in interest rates, loan terms, unexpected capital expenditures, and cash flow variability. Interest rate volatility can directly impact the cost of borrowing and, by extension, affect overall returns. Sponsors should be prepared with strategies such as interest rate caps or hedging instruments to mitigate this risk. Cash reserves also play a vital role in safeguarding against unforeseen expenses or cash flow disruptions, providing a buffer during periods of lower occupancy or short-term operational costs.

Regulatory risks involve any changes in local, state, or federal laws that could impact property operations or financial performance. Rent control measures, zoning law modifications, or shifts in tax policy can all create hurdles. Staying informed of legislative changes and fostering relationships with local regulatory bodies can help sponsors anticipate and respond effectively to such challenges. Environmental risks, though often unpredictable, are essential to consider as well. Natural disasters, hazardous materials, and pollution levels can all negatively impact the property. Insurance coverage, disaster preparedness plans, and compliance with environmental regulations help reduce these risks.

Tenant-related risks arise from tenant behavior and the property's tenant base. Non-payment of rent, property damage, or legal disputes with tenants can all strain finances and create operational challenges. Implementing a thorough tenant screening process and setting clear lease terms help mitigate these risks by attracting reliable, responsible tenants.

Market risks include changes in the broader economy, employment rates, disposable income, reduced rental demand, shifts in local employment opportunities, and population growth, all of which influence how your property will operate during a market cycle. The sponsor must also account for operational risks, which include inefficient management, which leads to higher vacancy rates, increased maintenance costs, tenant dissatisfaction, and employee turnover. Delayed or poor-quality repairs can lead to larger, more costly issues and tenant turnover.

Beyond identifying these risks, a well-rounded risk assessment includes creating contingency plans. This can mean setting aside financial reserves, securing appropriate insurance policies, or even maintaining alternative financing options. By approaching risk assessment as a proactive, ongoing process, sponsors can better protect their investments and navigate the multifamily market's inherent uncertainties. In summary, effective risk management isn't about eliminating all risks but preparing for them, thereby ensuring that the property remains viable and profitable even when faced with unexpected challenges.

Historical Income and Expense Comparison vs Sponsor Projection

This comparison is derived from the underwriting of the case study's subject property. It reflects a detailed analysis of the historical performance of the property in terms of income and expenses against the sponsor's projected figures during the acquisition phase.

Gross Potential Income: The total income the property could generate if fully occupied.

$1,335k vs $1,566k

Effective Gross Income: Adjusted for vacancy and collection losses.

$1,372k vs $1,508k

Net Operating Income (NOI): Effective gross income minus operating expenses.

$624k vs $830k

	T-12 Actual Financials		T-3 Annualized Income with T-12 Expenses		Year 1 Proforma - 2019		
	$641		$675			$881	
Market Rent	**$1,480,905**		**$1,485,760**		$1,649,160		
(Loss) / Gain to Lease	(145,145)		(130,408)		(152,555)	9.3%	
Value-Add Premiums					70,200		
Gross Potential Income	**$1,335,760**		**$1,355,352**		**$1,566,805**		
Vacancy Loss	(69,695)		(56,153)		(78,340)	5.0%	
Add. Vacancy Due To Renovation	-		-		(94,816)	6.1%	
Concessions / Other Economic Loss	(4,885)		(900)		(15,668)	1.0%	
Non-Revenue Units (model, employee)	(11,718)		(7,989)		-	0.0%	
Bad Debt	(49,820)		(25,831)		(31,336)	2.0%	
Effective Gross Income	**$1,199,642**		**$1,264,479**		**1,346,645**		
Other Income	99,085		70,702		87,532	6.5%	
Utility Reimbursement	73,951		84,188		73,951	$40	per mo avg
Total Income	**$1,372,678**		**$1,419,369**		**$1,508,128**		
Service Contracts, R&M, Turnover	91,867	589	91,867	589	100,000		641
Payroll	243,668	1,562	243,668	1,562	195,000		1,250
Marketing	25,160	161	25,160	161	23,000		147
Administration	48,094	308	48,094	308	22,000		141
Utilities	145,959	936	145,959	936	131,363		842
Management Fee	41,564	266	41,564	266	45,244	3.0%	290
Insurance	22,333	143	22,333	143	27,000		173
Real Estate Taxes	90,504	580	90,504	580	95,029		609
Total Operating Expenses	**709,149**	4,546	**709,149**	4,546	**638,636**		4,094
Lender Replacement Reserves	39,000	250	39,000	250	39,000		250
Total Expenses	**748,149**	4,796	**748,149**	4,796	**677,636**		4,344
Net Operating Income	**$624,529**		**$671,220**		**$830,492**		

Financial risk includes interest rate changes affecting mortgage payments and overall profitability. A rate increase can cause a loan default due to failure to meet debt obligations, leading to foreclosure and investment loss. To mitigate the financial risks involved, you need to focus on secured fixed-rate loans, maintain a strong DSCR, and maintain sufficient operational reserves to cover debt obligations during downturns. My recommendation is to have six months of operational expenses on hand.

Rent control, property taxes, and environmental standards can be examples of external noncontrollable risks that can impact profitability based on state and local ordinances. Non-compliance with existing regulations can lead to fines, legal issues, and increased operational costs. This can also apply to renovation permits and inspections so continue to stay informed about changes, engage legal counsel if necessary, and budget for potential costs. Let's not forget about natural disasters, floods, earthquakes, or hurricanes. Mold, asbestos, lead-based paint, and aluminum wiring are only a few of the environmental risks that can be mitigated through renovation, insurance, and proactive preparedness plans.

The largest risk to any multifamily property is the Rent Roll and tenants. Non-payment or late payment can affect cash flow and profitability; high vacancies reduce rental income while increasing marketing and turnover costs. To offset this risk, you must screen tenants thoroughly, offer competitive amenities, and maintain strong tenant relations to encourage lease renewals and stability. Always follow the Fair Housing Act while screening your prospective residents. Some companies require two and a half times the rental amount in income, while others require three times (Adams, 2021). One is obviously safer from a landlord's perspective but can limit the renter pool.

Utilizing a variety of tools and resources can significantly enhance the risk assessment process. Market research reports from sources, such as CoStar or Yardi Matrix can provide valuable data that can allow for informed decisions or identify additional risks. Engaging legal and environmental consultants is critical for conducting thorough assessments and staying compliant with all relevant regulations. These experts play a vital role in identifying potential issues that could impact the asset's success and providing a third-party verification of the property's viability. *Plus, the liability of title verification should be done by an attorney. The last thing you want is to buy a property that is not zoned properly.*

The final underwriting step involves stress testing the property and the sponsor's underwriting. By identifying potential risks, analyzing their impact, and developing mitigation strategies, sponsors can protect their investors and ensure long-term profitability.

From Terms to Trust

Once the underwriting process is complete and you have identified a suitable multifamily property, the next step is to make an offer. This phase consists of drafting a Letter of Intent (LOI). The LOI is a non-binding document that gives the basic terms and conditions of the proposed transaction. *We used to do this on a napkin or golf scorecard, but things have gotten much more formal.*

It serves as a preliminary agreement between the buyer and the seller, indicating the buyer's serious interest in purchasing the property. Sponsors generally prefer to include their track record, proof of funds, and ability to close along with their LOI submission. *If you have a loan quote before submitting your LOI, you can include that to demonstrate your ability to close.*

The deal points that you are looking to express to the other party include the purchase price, earnest money deposit, the projected due diligence timeframe, any financial contingencies needed, an intended closing date, and any other contingency required to complete the transaction purchase. An LOI is to express your intent and other deal points, which can cause issues during the purchase contract negotiation, so it is important to indicate the significant items in the beginning.

Through your underwriting, you should intimately know what your maximum purchase price will be on any transaction and at what point you need to walk away. The listing broker will, on occasion, provide pricing guidance called "Whisper Pricing" or "Market Pricing." The industry does this to remove any shock to the consumer during an email marketing blast or because the seller has an unrealistic expectation of value.

Determining the escrow deposit is entirely subjective to the market conditions, the supply and demand, the competition, and the seller. An initial deposit can generally be 1% of the purchase price. In a seller's market, a brokerage team is always pushing non-refundable deposits, also known as hard money. To this day, the ability to close the transaction trumps any hard money. Most groups that put up hard money have outs in other areas and have the funds to risk. Once you send in your escrow, regardless of your DD or Contingencies, the seller can always make it extensively difficult to recover the funds.

Creating a reasonable and confident due diligence timeline that is competitive can be tricky. During a DD timeline, the buyer can conduct thorough inspections of the property, both physical and operational. Some groups walk a sample of a property, 10%-20%. If you do not walk all the units, you will be sad eventually.

The generally accepted timeline used to be 30 days for due diligence and 60 days to close, totaling 90 days. Market-dependent, this can run concurrently, speeding up a timeline, and in a very aggressive market, the timeframe can be shrunk to 45 or even 30 days from PSA signing to closing, but that commitment requires a tremendous amount of coordination.

There is always an opportunity to stick out during the bidding process by reducing your timeframes or having no due diligence. We have utilized the time frame between an accepted LOI and negotiating a Purchase and Sale Agreement (PSA) to accomplish our DD and wired escrow funds upon the signing of a PSA with a 45-day close.

Including a financial contingency is another way to protect your escrow funds but can diminish your offer's strength. It involves placing criteria on the seller to hit certain benchmarks during the contract term to ensure that the property qualifies for the loan through closing. Sellers and brokers are not fans of a financial contingency, but I have found that surety of close generally outweighs this issue. In a market where debt facilities are prevalent, you may have more comfort in risking your escrow funds, knowing that you can get the loan.

After the submission of an LOI, there is a waiting game while the broker group consolidates the offerings and presents the package of offers to the selling group. There is sometimes an opportunity to circumvent this wildly annoying process that we call "Best and Final," where the listing broker calls all the prospective buyers to solicit a second offer. This offer will be higher or have more stringent terms or removals of contingencies—leave yourself some wiggle room for negotiation. You may be negotiating with yourself, so be careful.

Once a second round of offers has been submitted along with track records and business plans, you can be chosen to have an interview call with the seller. Generally, a broker prefers to avoid putting two principals on the phone, but in some cases, you can win or lose a property by showing your ability to close the transaction.

Remember, we are all working towards the same goal. You want to buy the property, and they want to sell it. There are plenty of times during the entire process that it will feel as if both the buyer and seller are at war. These are the critical moments to have a skilled commercial real estate broker capable of managing their clients.

Celebrating the Close

Congratulations! You have been selected to purchase the chosen property. You got that call from the broker telling you that you now have the opportunity to do all the things you said you would in your LOI. Your reputation will define your future, so make certain you can complete what you claim to be able to do.

Now is when the real work begins: risking and spending money. The funds will eventually be allocated to the sponsor's equity account. Still, a sponsor will often secure the asset with personal funds, engage transactional council, submit a loan application, schedule due diligence, wire escrow deposits, and order required lender third-party reports. You must spend money to make money, but these transactional costs can increase quickly, and if you do not close the transaction, the costs will be your responsibility.

Following the acceptance of the LOI, the next step is to negotiate the PSA, a legally binding contract that formalizes the terms of the sale. The major points in a PSA expand upon the LOI, providing a detailed amount to be paid and the payment schedule. In most cases, the full amount is paid to the selling party at closing, but in some cases, a seller may decide to carry back a portion of equity or Joint Venture (JV) in the future transaction.

Both the seller and the buyer provide each other with representations and warranties. These are statements from the seller and buyer regarding the condition of the property and entity. In the PSA, a named person provides the specific knowledge points and if you are not careful, the person may not have relevant knowledge that you need. An example is an out-of-state owner selling a property in Phoenix that hasn't traveled due to COVID. It is possible to have a property with local ordinance violations known to the onsite team while the contractually named contact may be blissfully unaware. There is a benefit to deniability.

Be sure to include in the PSA the full property description, address, legal description, total unit count, acreage, and all personal or property assets included in the sale. The personal or property assets can consist of maintenance equipment, appliances, office desks, computers, or digital assets. Other significant points in a PSA include a detailed closing procedure, title transfer, funds disbursement, and default provisions. While an LOI may be one or two pages, a PSA can be extensive when attorneys are involved. Great deal making transactional attorneys are hard to find but worth it—pay them.

After the purchase agreement is signed, the due diligence timeline, if there is one, begins. Occasionally, it is possible to delay the signing of the PSA for a few days to firm up your loan application and coordinate the DD teams. This can also be a negotiating tactic, but the longer it drags out, the more frustrated the seller can become, causing the broker to shop your offer to other potential groups. Don't forget that the LOI is non-binding until the PSA is signed and escrow funds are deposited, and time kills all deals.

As you complete the purchase agreement, begin securing the financing. Executing your loan application is a part of acquiring a multifamily property. The process involves submitting detailed information about the existing property and the borrower to the selected potential lenders and preparing the financial documents in advance, including personal and business financial statements and tax returns. The lender will require an appraisal of the property, which a third party completes, to verify the asset's value against which to lend. During the loan application process, the lender will inspect the property, seek a constant update of operational financials, and search the backgrounds of all the borrowing principals participating in the transaction.

The transition from making an offer to due diligence

entails several critical steps and funding to ensure the property is thoroughly vetted and financially viable. By taking the time to carefully prepare the LOI, PSA, DD, and loan application, sponsors can effectively manage the risks and move towards a successful acquisition.

Lessons from the Field

The Subject Property was surrounded by a thriving local economy, with significant job growth driven by diverse industries. This economic vitality was a positive indicator of sustained rental demand. The area's diverse demographic profile, including many working professionals and growing families, indicates a robust rental market. The Subject Property was situated in a market with a healthy balance of supply and demand. The area had high occupancy rates and low vacancies, signaling solid rental demand.

The property's competitive analysis revealed that nearby properties had high occupancy rates and competitive rental rates, supporting the potential for rent growth and high occupancy.

Interior and Exterior Renovation Scope

Classic

# of Units	Rent	Sq Ft	Rent PSF	Rent Monthly	Rent Annualized
12	$815	600	$1.36	$9,780	$117,360
12	$830	600	$1.38	$9,960	$119,520
11	$935	750	$1.25	$10,659	$127,908
11	$950	750	$1.27	$10,830	$129,960

Throughout
- Patch all walls and trim in preparation for paint; paint entire interior, two colors, colors TBD by owner
- Replace all door knobs
- New thermostat
- Remove and Replace all plumbing to meet Green requirements

Flooring
- Replace as needed

Kitchen
- Used appliances taken from Upgraded or Renovated units

Total Projected Cost Per Unit (Completed by Operations)

Total Units	Total Cost	Total Project Cost
47	$2,500	$117,000

Interior Summary

Unit Count	Cost/Unit	Total Cost
47	$2,500	$117,000
78	$8,000	$624,000
31	$15,000	$468,000
Subtotal		**$1,209,000**
Contingency	$775	$120,900
156	**$8,525**	**$1,329,900**

Upgraded

# of Units	Rent	Sq Ft	Rent PSF	Rent Monthly	Rent Annualized
20	$915	600	$1.53	$18,300	$219,600
20	$930	600	$1.55	$18,600	$223,200
19	$1,035	750	$1.38	$19,665	$235,980
19	$1,050	750	$1.40	$19,950	$239,400

Throughout
- Patch all walls in preparation for paint; paint entire interior, two colors, colors TBD by owner
- Replace all interior doors with Cheayanne Panel Doors
- New appliances (Stove, Microwave, Fridge, Dishwasher)
- Remove and Replace all plumbing fixtures, toilets, and valves
- Remove and Replace all base board
- Remove and Replace all lighting fixtures
- Scrape popcorn ceiling, texture, and paint
- New thermostat

Flooring
- Replace carpet with new carpet

Kitchen
- Refinish existing cabinets
- Install cabinet door hardware
- Remove and replace countertops with new laminate
- Replace sink
- Replace plumbing
- Re-Install Garbage Disposal

Bathroom(s)
- Replace toilet
- Refinish existing cabinets
- Install cabinet door hardware
- Replace tub/shower valve and trim
- Resurface tub

Total Projected Cost Per Unit (Compleated by Third Party)

Total Units	Total Cost	Total Project Cost
78	$8,000	$624,000

Renovated

# of Units	Rent	Sq Ft	Rent PSF	Rent Monthly	Rent Annualized
8	$1,015	600	$1.69	$8,120	$97,440
8	$1,030	600	$1.72	$8,240	$98,880
8	$1,135	750	$1.51	$8,626	$103,512
8	$1,150	750	$1.53	$8,740	$104,880

Throughout
- Patch all walls in preparation for paint; paint entire interior, two colors, colors TBD by owner
- Replace all interior doors with Cheayanne Panel Doors
- New appliances (Stove, Microwave, Fridge, Dishwasher)
- Remove and Replace all plumbing fixtures, toilets, and valves
- Remove and Replace all base board
- Remove and Replace all lighting fixtures
- Scrape popcorn ceiling, texture, and paint
- Remove and Replace all electrical switches and outlets
- Remove and Replace all mechanical registers
- New thermostat

Flooring
- Replace all with vinyl plank

Kitchen
- Remove and Replace cabinets with new boxes
- Install cabinet door hardware
- Remove and replace countertops with new hard surface tops
- Replace sink
- Replace plumbing
- Replace Garbage Disposal

Bathroom(s)
- Replace toilet
- Remove and Replace vanity and sink
- Install Cabinet door hardware
- Replace tub/shower valve and trim
- Resurface tub and replace surround

Total Projected Cost Per Unit (Completed by Third Party)

Total Units	Total Cost	Total Project Cost
31	$15,000	$468,000

Exterior Renovation

General Conditions/Supervision — $7,800
- Pest Control: Treat all buildings including clubhouse for subterranean termits with a 2 year warranty. Subject to general terms and conditions and renewal annually thereafter.

Concrete — $7,800
- Replace steps (just treads)
- Remove and Replace concrete walks where trip hazards are identified

Parking Lots — $46,800
- Mill and replace existing 3" asphalt
- Seal Coat - Two coats PPM Sealer with crack sealing
- Striping

Pool — $31,200
- Acid wash waterline tile, install new grabrails
- Demo some of the decking and pour new concrete, resurface all
- Install new equipment and above ground plumbing

Landscape/Common Areas — $78,000
- Remove and replace BBQ, Replace shade sail
- Replace soccer field goals and netting, repair and replace irrigation
- 4' Chain link for dog park area and wash station

Roofs — $85,800
- Remove devris, powerwash flat roofs, apply mastic to penetrations, repair flashing as needed, replace 58 tiles, apply stucco over parapet walls to repair cracks

Wrought Iron Fence — $117,000
- Replace pool fencing and gates with glass in specific areas
- New automated system with card readers, replace fencing to east
- Replace all patio wood gates with new wrought iron gates

Finishes — $234,000
- Remove painted tile, lathe and stucco with smooth sand finish
- Repair or replace as needed wood deck spindles and paint
- Paint exterior (3-color scheme TBD by owner)

Electrical — $23,400
- Removal of all existing security lighting, run new conduit for security, install all new wall packs (includes fixtures), indtallation of new duplex exterior outlets, demo and install of carport lights

Additional Category — $23,400
- Branding
- Fire and safety (all new extinguishers, cabinets, and detectors)
- Architectural and engineering

Additional Category — $85,800
- Clubhouse renovation allocation
- Maintenance shop allowance

Specialities — $31,200
- Gate automation
- Signage for the property

Projected Cost Per Unit (Completed by Third Party)

Total Units	Per Unit Cost	Subtotal Project Cost
156	$5,000	$780,000

Contingency

Total Units	Per Unit Cost	Total Contingency
156	$600	$93,600

Total Cost Per Unit (Completed by Third Party)

Total Units	Total Per Unit Cost	Total Project Cost
156	$5,600	$873,600

Adapting to Variables

- **Sensitivity analysis:** Different scenarios were modeled to assess the impact of changes in key assumptions, such as rent growth, vacancy rates, and expense growth on the property's financial performance.

The initial projections for the Subject Property estimated a steady increase in rental income due to strong market demand and planned property improvements.

For the Subject Property, a comprehensive analysis was conducted to evaluate different financing options and structure the deal effectively. The process began with considering a traditional mortgage, which offered stability through a fixed interest rate, giving a reliable financing option for the property. Ultimately, it was decided that the returns provided to the investors would not be sufficient due to the lower funding availability of 65% LTV funding and zero renovation funding.

Government-backed loans, such as those from Fannie Mae, Freddie Mac, and HUD, were evaluated for competitive terms, although they required more stringent compliance and documentation. During our proposed business plan, the property would be reduced in occupancy to accommodate the renovation component. The security of government-backed loans is generally sacrificed by sponsorship when a property requires drastic repositioning.

Finally, we considered a short-term bridge loan, which, while offering the potential for a larger loan amount and higher return, also came with increased risk, particularly if paired with an inexperienced sponsor. Each financing option was carefully assessed to determine the best fit for the investment strategy and risk tolerance of the stakeholders involved.

After an extensive market analysis to maximize the return to our investor group, we selected a Bridge Loan that provided 80% of the Purchase Price (PP) of the asset and 100% of our projected renovations for a total loan amount of $14,400k. The remainder of the project equity was sourced from accredited investors, personal funds, family, and friends.

Below is an example of the general deal points from the three bridge loan groups for the subject property. The quotes are focused on loan terms provided by three different bridge lending groups.

	Lender 1	Selected Lender	Lender 3
Total Budget:	$18,130,989	$18,130,989	$18,130,989
Loan Amount:	$13,660,000	$14,400,000	$13,660,000
LTC:	75%	80% PP; 100% renovations	75%
Initial Funding:	$11,039,200	$11,800,000	$11,039,000
Origination Fee:	1.0%	1.0%	1.0%
Exit Fee:	1.0%	0.5%	0.5%
Index Rate:	1 Mo Libor	1 Mo Libor	1 Mo Libor
Spread:	3.45%	3.15%	3.20%
All In Rate:	5.95%	5.65%	5.70%
Amortization:	Interest Only	Interest Only	Interest Only
Minimum Interest:	18 Months	18 month YM	18 Months
Term:	36 Months	36 months	36 months
Extension:	2 x 12 months each	2 x 12 months each	1 x 12 months
Extension Fee:	0.25% first; 0.50% for second	0.25% each	0.50%

The selected lender indicated an interest rate of Libor +3.15%, providing a 5.65% interest rate at the time of purchase that will increase throughout the transaction. To be conservative, a total rate of 5.90% was used in the initial underwriting. The repayment schedule is calculated over a 30-year amortization, interest-only. The loan would be due in 36 months, giving the sponsor enough time to reposition the property and refinance with long-term fixed-rate debt or dispose of the property.

If you have chosen to use a floating rate loan, the lender will indicate a floor, which is the lowest the interest rate will ever be, regardless of whether Libor reduces. The floor is shown in the loan documents or is defined by the interest rate upon loan funding. The availability of negotiating a ceiling is dependent on the track record and existing relationship with the lending facility. A lender rarely considers it.

Regarding extensions, your property must maintain the specified DSCR during the loan term. When renovating the asset, income can be reduced, lowering this ratio. While this is generally not an issue during the transaction, you may find that you do not qualify for the extensions provided in your loan documents due to the execution of the business plan.

For the Subject Property, an LLC was established to manage the investment, providing liability protection and operational flexibility. The operating agreement outlined working members' and limited partners' roles and responsibilities, ensuring transparent governance and decision-making processes. Often, an Organization Chart can summarize the ownership structure of the LLC.

Below is the Organization Chart used for the Subject Property. The chart provides a detailed breakdown of entities and personal ownership percentages. The gray box at the top is the SPE created to hold the title to the asset and sign the loan. Below the Borrower tier is the Management entity responsible for executing the business plan and the Partner entity that contributed a prorated equity share.

[redacted]

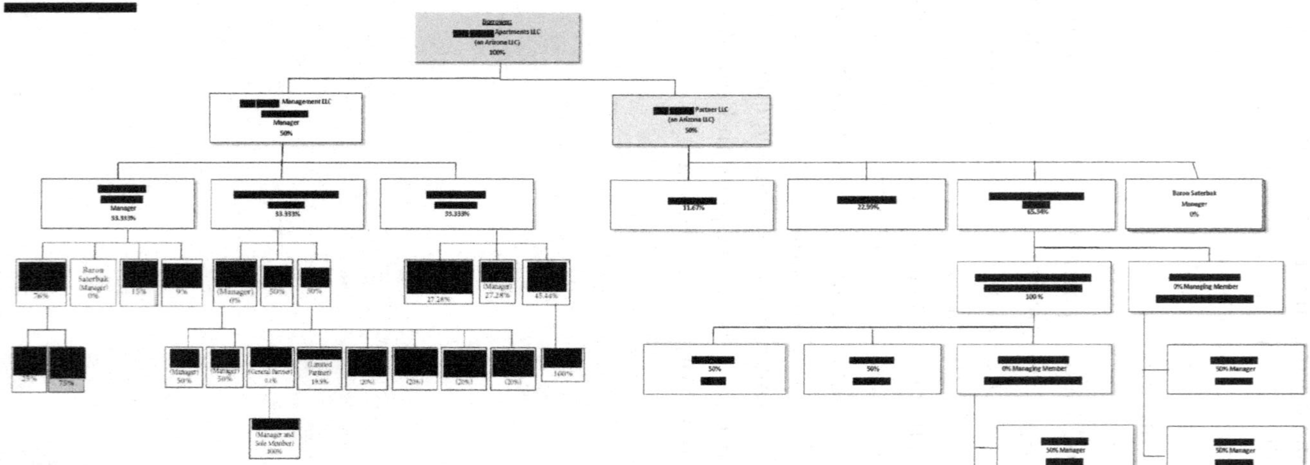

[redacted]

In conclusion, underwriting is a critical element of any real estate project, particularly when it comes to property repositioning. It's the phase where the viability of a deal is evaluated, not just in terms of financial but also the potential risks and rewards. Understanding how lenders think while underwriting helps align project goals with funding options. This process scrutinizes every detail, from market conditions to borrower credentials, so that the project has a strong foundation for success. A thorough underwriting process not only helps secure financing but also sets a clear roadmap for project milestones, keeping the investment on track.

By now, it should be evident that successful underwriting hinges on several factors: accurate financial projections, a solid management team, proper documentation, and alignment with the lender's risk appetite. Borrowers who anticipate lender concerns and present a clear, economically viable proposition increase their chances of approval. Yet, underwriting is just one part of the broader real estate journey.

Securing financing is only the first hurdle. The next crucial step in the process is due diligence. Before committing to a project, investors and lenders need to ensure that everything about the property, both physically and financially, holds up to scrutiny. Enter the due diligence phase, where everything from structural soundness to the reliability of Rent Rolls is verified, mitigating risks and confirming the property's true value. Without proper due diligence, even the most promising underwriting can unravel, leading to costly oversights or project failures.

Due diligence is the process of thoroughly investigating all aspects of a property before finalizing a transaction. This phase is necessary to verify that no major issues have been overlooked that could derail the project's success. From physical inspections to financial audits, due diligence examines every detail to validate the property's condition, profitability, and compliance with regulatory requirements.

While underwriting focuses on the financial potential of a

property, due diligence digs into the reality. Structural issues, unresolved legal matters, environmental concerns, or inaccurate tenant information can all be red flags. The goal of due diligence is to confirm that the property's physical and financial state matches what was represented during the underwriting process, protecting investors from unforeseen risks.

In the next sections, we will explore the key components of due diligence, how to identify potential red flags, and the critical role this phase plays in safeguarding your investment.

CHAPTER 3

Mastering Due Diligence

Imagine you're about to buy a car. You wouldn't hand over your money without taking it for a test drive, examining its condition, and reviewing its history. Investing in a multifamily property follows a similar principle. Before you commit to a deal, conduct thorough due diligence—the process of verifying the property's financial, legal, and physical condition so that it aligns with your investment goals.

In the world of multifamily asset management, due diligence is more than just a safety check. It's a safeguard against unpleasant surprises down the road, from hidden structural issues to unexpected market shifts.

This chapter will guide you through the key elements of the due diligence process, exploring everything from reviewing financial statements to conducting physical inspections and environmental assessments. At the end of this chapter, you'll understand not only how to conduct effective due diligence but also how it can empower you to negotiate better deals and manage risks confidently in a competitive market.

The Due Diligence (DD) process is a comprehensive evaluation conducted before acquiring a multifamily property to ensure the investment is sound and identify potential risks or liabilities. This process involves meticulously examining various aspects of the property, including its financial performance, legal standing, physical condition, and environmental impact.

Due Diligence is the beginning of verifying your assumptions during the underwriting process. You can include a list of your required DD items to be provided by the seller in the PSA so that everyone knows your requests in advance. Generally speaking, getting the extensive list of items indicated on the Due Diligence Checklist provided later in this section is complex. Unfortunately, the squeaky wheel usually gets grease.

Use every opportunity to mitigate the risk by identifying potential issues affecting the property to fully understand the current state and verify that the sponsor's vision is attainable in the projected timeframe. There is sometimes an opportunity to renegotiate the Purchase and Sale Agreement (PSA) and Purchase Price (PP) during the DD period. Uncovering deficiencies or issues can help negotiate better pricing or request repairs and adjustments. The Due Diligence period is your final opportunity to negotiate any remaining concerns of unforeseen financial burdens, including mechanics' liens found in the title report.

Brokers and sellers disdain a trade of the PP and will vet a sponsor's previous record with other brokerage houses. However, there are times that an adjustment to the purchase price is warranted. In the past we have had a vendor camera the sewer lines. When we received the report, the entire property needed the sewage lines replaced, causing upwards of 1.5M in unforeseen repairs. In that transaction, we needed a adjustment, leading to an offer to either reduce the property's price or terminate the deal. We did purchase the property but had to vacate the entire property, building by building while replacing underground lines; it was extensive.

Reviewing the title documents, lease agreements, and zoning of the property to verify compliance with all local, state, and federal regulations to avoid any legal impediments post-purchase is part of the legal DD. The Subject Property's title work indicated an access easement that would need to be removed by the sponsor during the transaction. Lending facilities have different nuances as it relates to physical asset. An example being government-backed loans don't like barbed wire on perimeter fencing and will require you to take it down before funding.

The easement was a minor issue in the grand scheme because of the bridge loan. If we had selected a government-backed loan in the underwriting process, the easement would have been a negotiating point for the seller to remove so we could close the asset with agency debt. Due to the local processing times, removing an easement can take anywhere from 30 days to 12 months.

The physical component of Due Diligence requires the inspection of the physical asset, including structure, systems, units, and maintenance needs. If you work with a competent management team, you can coordinate due diligence inspections over one or two days, depending on the asset size. When inspecting the property, take photos, inspect every unit, and make notes; you will not remember everything. The extensive inspection notations are shown in the case study QR code as we indicate which units will be renovated first and to what tier of renovation. To ensure efficiency, renovate the most damaged units first for the most significant Return on Investment (ROI).

The unit walk is needed to verify and confirm the accuracy of the Rent Roll, which is why it's essential to inspect every apartment. For example, in a 130-unit complex in the Midwest, the January rent roll indicated that 19 units were vacant. However, a physical inspection revealed much higher numbers than expected. A total of 63 units were found to be either vacant, delinquent and vacant, or delinquent, under eviction, and vacant, amounting to 48% of the units.

Property Historical Vacancy	
January 31, 2018 Rent Roll	
Vacant Units	19
April 4, 2018 Rent Roll	
Vacant Units	31

Additional Vacancy Calcualtion	
Vacancy Difference between January and April Rent Roll	12
Additional Vacancy with Evictions, Apartments with Unpaid Rent, Physical Vacant listed as Occupied	32
Monthly Additional Vacancy	$35,080

Unit Reduction	44	42	40	38	36	34	32	30	28	26	24
Month	May-18	Jun-18	Jul-18	Aug-18	Sep-18	Oct-18	Nov-18	Dec-18	Jan-19	Feb-19	Mar-19
GPR	$35,080	$33,485	$31,891	$30,296	$28,702	$27,107	$25,513	$23,918	$22,324	$20,729	$19,135
Unit Reduction	22	20	18	16	14	12	10	8	6	4	2
Month	Apr-19	May-19	May-19	May-19	May-19	May-19	May-19	May-19	May-19	May-19	May-19
GPR	$17,540	$15,945	$14,351	$12,756	$11,162	$9,567	$7,973	$6,378	$4,784	$3,189	$1,595

Total Vacancy Cost	**$403,420**

Turn Cost Analysis Based on Physical Walk 2/21/18 Indicated Units	
Flooring Replacement (32 Units) (Carpet Showcase $1,400/Unit)	$44,800
Flooring Cleaning (12 Units)(Dans Carpet Cleaning $100/Unit)	$1,200
Painting (GWE Quote $500/Unit)	$22,000
Maintenance ($275/Unit)	$12,100
Total Turn Cost Analysis	**$80,100**

Water Main Damage and Estimated Repairs	
Description	**Cost**
Excavate and replace concrete and fix water main leak at units 37-40	$15,000
Excavate and replace concrete and fix water main leak between units 70 and 82	$5,000
Total	**$20,000**

Total Vacancy and Turn Adjustment Since PSA	**$503,520**

This discovery prompted an immediate revision of the business plan, necessitating additional equity and the involvement of a local bank. We focused on the extra units beyond the initial 19 listed in the January rent roll, which had been the basis for our original underwriting. We adjusted the plan to reduce the additional 44 units found to be vacant, initially listed as occupied, by 2 units per month alongside the regular leasing efforts. We also accounted for the units requiring improvements that were not initially disclosed by the broker or seller. Following extensive negotiations, we secured a $500k reduction in the purchase price based on these inspections.

During the physical inspections, we also need to turn our attention to the environmental inspections that will occur and will be demanded by the lender during the DD process. These inspections are essential for uncovering any hidden ecological liabilities that could significantly impact the property's value and future operations.

There are different levels of environmental inspection, and if the first inspection returns any minor concerns, more extensive testing will be required. The initial Phase I is a lesser report if no historical concerns are related to the property. An additional inspection can be very invasive to the existing asset. If the property once had any chemical spills, underground storage tanks, or any other external factors, a Phase II report will be initiated and completed.

A structured approach helps identify potential red flags and adds significant value to the investment by ensuring that all aspects of the property are thoroughly vetted. The following sections will delve deeper into each component, providing detailed guidelines and best practices for conducting a comprehensive due diligence process.

Inspecting the Foundation

Physical due diligence consists of a thorough assessment of the property's physical condition to pinpoint any issues affecting its value, operational efficiency, or safety. This process helps investors plan for necessary repairs, renovations, and maintenance to ensure the investment's long-term viability. Understanding the current state of the building's infrastructure allows for a reallocation of renovation funds to complete the business plan.

The property inspection phase involves hiring professional inspectors to evaluate the different aspects of the infrastructure and determine the remaining life cycle of major building systems, including the building exterior, common areas, mechanical systems, and safety protocols. The exterior and common areas focus on the building's structure, assessing the foundation, walls, roofing, and other structural elements. A roof that included a 20-year warranty but was installed 15 years ago will have an indicated life of 5 remaining years and will need to be replaced before the future sale or refinance of the asset. Additionally, the condition of the landscaping and irrigation, parking areas, walkways, and drainage systems are evaluated along with common areas, such as lobbies, hallways, recreational facilities, and other shared spaces.

Finding the correct vendor for a mechanical systems inspection cannot be neglected when it comes to understanding the potential exposure. HVAC systems are checked for functionality and efficiency, while plumbing inspectors focus on piping, fixtures, water heaters, and sewage systems. Electrical systems are evaluated for safety, including electrical wiring, panels, outlets, and lighting conditions. The available power in older assets can struggle to keep up with today's demands. Adding microwaves, dishwashers, garbage disposals, washers, and dryers can require replacing the interior and exterior electrical boxes to increase the power from the regional provider to the resident. Keep in mind that the addition of power will need local inspection and permit coordination.

Safety and compliance must also be evaluated. Fire safety measures are reviewed to confirm that alarms, sprinkler systems, and fire extinguishers are in working order and comply with local regulations. Security systems, such as locks, cameras, internal lighting, and exterior lighting, are assessed for their condition and effectiveness.

As a notation, if your renovation scope includes adjusting any entrances or exits to the facility, you will need to pay specific attention to the asset's compliance with the Americans with Disabilities Act (ADA) and other relevant accessibility standards, ensuring the property is accessible to all individuals.

While the hired professionals complete the property's physical condition inspections, the selected management team should be focused on the detailed inspection of individual units, assessing their condition, and identifying necessary repairs. Unit walks involve inspecting all the living spaces to verify they meet safety and habitability standards for the existing and future residents. The management team must focus on structural integrity, plumbing and electrical, fixtures and appliances, and safety and compliance.

Furthermore, the management and maintenance team will continue to focus on the structural integrity of the unit interiors, including checking walls, floors, and ceilings for signs of damage, including cracks, water stains, or mold. Inspecting the unit plumbing and electrical systems will involve testing plumbing fixtures for leaks and proper function while making sure electrical switches and outlets are operational and safe.

Extensive notations are priceless while the team moves through the property and DD process. Understanding precisely the condition of each appliance, and if the kitchen fixtures are in working order will inform any future renovation scope. This process will also verify the count of appliances like stoves and refrigerators to match the personal property list in the PSA.

The team must also test safety and compliance items, take special care of them, and consider the existing residents. Smoke and carbon monoxide detectors, in addition to other safety devices, are installed and functioning. Bring 9-volt batteries with you. The residents will appreciate a working smoke detector even though you don't own the property. This is truly your first opportunity to have a first impression with the residents and existing staff.

The extensive data provided by all the associated professionals should give you the information you need to confirm that you are willing to move forward with the transaction purchase or that the property has more infrastructure risk than was initially understood to be required. The Subject Property case study highlights the importance of detailed physical due diligence and how it contributes to successfully managing and enhancing a multifamily asset. Be prepared to sacrifice real-time at the property during the DD process to get it right. My mother always said, "Don't buy something unless you are willing to live there because you might."

Legal Safeguards

During the DD process, a laundry list of legal items must be verified. A comprehensive review of legal documents and contracts is done to identify potential issues or liabilities. A comprehensive legal due diligence process confirms that investors are aware of the property's legal status and can take necessary actions to mitigate risks.

The critical components of the legal due diligence process entail reviewing the title documents, lease agreements, zoning and land use compliance, environmental compliance, pending litigation or disputes, vendor contracts, and insurance policies. Engaging a professional transactional council will give the stakeholders an added assurance level during this phase of the due diligence process.

The purchase and sale agreement indicates the title company conducting the transaction coordination, funding, escrow, and documentation recording. Over time, you may prefer to work with a title company or a specific transaction agent. It may not be worth losing a transaction over a title company discussion with the seller, but I can assure you there are transaction coordinators who *should* and some who *shouldn't*. A title company will provide you with a title report and insurance.

You need to get a title report to verify the property's ownership and identify any encumbrances, such as liens, easements, or covenants. Knowing if there are existing mechanics' liens on the property can indicate the financial health of the current ownership. At the same time, any undisclosed land use restrictions related to age (55+) or resident income restrictions, often referred to as Low-Income Housing Tax Credits (LIHTC), can adjust the value of the physical asset.

After reviewing the title work, the title company will give you title insurance to show you the specific items they are willing to defend if someone were to challenge your ownership of the asset at a given time. This will include utility easements and other historical items that affect the chain of title.

Review all existing lease agreements to understand the terms and conditions, including but not limited to rent amounts, lease duration, and tenant responsibilities. It will offer the new management team a baseline for managing the current residents while transitioning to a new set of leasing documents. Ensure the leases comply with the local tenant laws and regulations to protect the landlord and tenant's rights.

Over the years, states have provided different criteria for leasing apartments. While some require that the on-site manager have a real estate license, other states have little to no requirements for the on-site team. This can cause a large discrepancy in lease documents, from a form-fill PDF document to a custom-drafted document with addendum after addendum. Be sure to read every word and know the document you are adopting as new ownership while transitioning the asset.

Verify that the property complies with the current zoning and land use regulations. For this purpose, you will need to check for any zoning changes or variances that can affect the property's use. There are both conforming and non-conforming uses. A conforming use matches the currently available options for the existing zoning. On the other hand, a non-conforming use property may have had the zoning changed by the local municipality over the years but after the property was built. A non-conforming asset is generally not a zoning violation but can become an issue if extensive renovations are planned. Yes, it is also a possibility that a city can change the zoning for your property and not notify you. That is why you need to investigate, and research planned or potential developments in the immediate and surrounding areas that can easily impact the property's value, from entertainment venues and restaurants to power stations and prisons.

I am touching briefly on the environmental regulations and assessments here as there is an extensive focus in a few pages that goes into more detail. Conduct a Phase I and, if needed, a Phase II Environmental Site Assessment (ESA) to identify any environmental hazards or contamination issues. Make certain the property complies with all local, state, and federal environmental regulations. Over these years, there have been very few issues regarding this component in direct relation to existing multifamily properties. However, the redevelopment and repurposing of many locations nationwide continue to reinforce this report's needs. An example being an old textile factory being converted to apartments.

Investigate any ongoing or past litigation involving the property or current owner. This includes lawsuits, administrative actions, or regulatory investigations. Review the dispute resolution mechanism outlined in the existing property's contracts and leases. Be on the lookout for mechanic leans or partnership disputes.

A review of all vendor and service contracts will include management, maintenance, and utility providers. The property buyer will generally have the option to assume or refuse any contracts on the property. This will be easier in some cases rather than in others. Laundry leases are notoriously tricky to terminate with automatic 5-year contract renewals and termination notice requirements limited to 1 year before the ending of a 5-year renewal but not less than 9 months before a renewal date. In contrast, a landscaping contract may have a 30-day cancelation policy. The PSA will define whose responsibility it is to terminate the contract, but once you have indicated the ones you are willing to accept, the contracts will transition with the asset to the new ownership group.

Examining the existing insurance policy to confirm adequate coverage for property damage, liability, and other risks through closing. Anything can happen over the PSA timeline, including the destruction of the asset by natural disasters. Be sure that you understand the terms and conditions of the existing policies, like the deductible, coverage limits, and exclusions. You can also ensure that the coverage matches lender requirements.

In 2021, in Arizona, a sponsor could reasonably assume that a property would require $250 PUPA solely for insurance. Due to the adjustment in insurance criteria, any asset built before 2000 has been placed in another class, raising the previous underwriting estimates from $250 to $500 PUPA. Nothing has changed on the asset or the risk profile, and that $250 PUPA difference has been passed on to the residents as a rent increase (est. $20 per month). We will continue to get into this further in the operational section.

This may feel overwhelming. I can assure you there are tools and resources to help you through this process. You can hire experienced real estate attorneys to review all legal documents and guarantee compliance with applicable laws. Likewise, you can work with reputable title companies to obtain title reports and secure title insurance. Finally, you can use a comprehensive checklist, so that all aspects of the legal due diligence are covered.

Sponsors can mitigate risk and protect their investments by reviewing legal documents, confirming compliance with regulations, and identifying potential legal issues. The case study will highlight the importance of a thorough process and how it contributes to successfully acquiring a multifamily property.

Verifying the Numbers

The next phase of the due diligence process is about thoroughly reviewing the property's financial records to verify its financial health and identify any discrepancies. This process makes sure that investors understand the property's economic performance and potential risks clearly. This review will verify or dispute the previously provided marketing materials, financial documents, and sponsor underwriting assumptions. Verifying the income, expenses, existing loans or new loan requirements, and property tax records will provide a complete view of the property's long-term potential.

Financial statements, Rent Rolls, expenses, debt, and tax records are all part of the review process. You may think *I have the T12 and the RR from my underwriting. What else do I need?* The bank statement from the property shows the deposits correlating to the property's stated collections. Be sure to review the balance sheets of the property's assets, liabilities, and equity, if available, and examine the cash flow statements to evaluate the property's liquidity and cash flow management.

Financial documents can be maintained in an accrual or cash accounting format. Suppose the current asset maintains an accrual T12. In that case, the property financials may show monthly payments to utility companies but only receive invoices semi-monthly or, in extreme cases, annually. The physical cash may be in the account but already allocated in the accrual accounting for future invoices. A cash statement should indicate the money that has come in and gone out each month, which carries its flaws as it relates to late or bulk payments.

The Rent Roll is the beating heart of the asset. Verify the accuracy of the current Rent Roll, such as tenant names, lease terms, rental rates, and payment histories. Review the historical and current occupancy rates to gauge tenant turnover and stability. While the management team is onsite for the physical inspection, an office team should verify the current Rent Roll with a lease audit.

This is a time-consuming process and can involve pulling twenty-year-old individual paper files from the depts of a manager's office to complete. The selected lender will require a certified Rent Roll to close on the property; the buyer must sign off that they are confident in the report's accuracy. There is no third-party verification of this critical financial verification to ensure enough funds are available to cover the debt obligation. Checking invoices, contracts, and payment records can verify operational expenses in many ways. Maintenance repair records will present a unique perspective of the property's reoccurring maintenance concerns and general upkeep costs that may not arise otherwise. It will also signal the repetitive decision to repair with in-house staff or replace with new. The capital expenditures made on the property should be cataloged for review to provide insight into the property improvements and long-term longevity.

In certain situations, a property's debt may be assumable. It means that the new buyer can take over the existing loan. This can be beneficial due to a lower-than-market fixed interest rate and can also be a complete nightmare to transition from the current seller to a new ownership group. So, analyze the terms and conditions of any assumable existing loans, including interest rates, amortization schedules, and covenants. Regardless of a loan assumption or a new loan on the property, you must calculate the DSCR to verify the property's income is sufficient to cover the debt obligations.

Property taxes are different by state, county, and city. Review property tax assessments and payments to verify their accuracy and identify any discrepancies. As a point of consideration, different states will adjust the assessed value of an asset to the newly paid purchase price, increasing the property taxes in a compensatory way. An unknown property tax increase risk can ruin a transaction and any profitability. Therefore, make sure you know the property tax policy regarding the property's location, and always seek professional guidance in this category. During the property tax review, you may encounter a tax lien due to nonpayment by the current ownership. The title company should ensure this is satisfied upon the sale and will be debited to the seller on the closing statement. Make a note of it for later if it does not appear organically on the closing statement; we are all human, and a good transaction coordinator is hard to find since they're usually stretched very thin.

Do a final review of the vendor contract and service agreements. Reviewing and examining the contract with the individual providers can help you gain insights into the existing relationship and anything that is different from the contract. Be aware that sitting with a landscaping or cleaning company to review the existing contract and expectations is always easier than a cable company or laundry lease contract.

The financial due diligence process is mainly dependent on the sponsorship. While some professionals will give you tax insight and transactional counsel, most groups rely on their personal experience and the management team's experience to confirm this process. Some properties have complete and verifiable financials at the push of a button through management and accounting software, while others still function with paper binders and Excel to track their Rent Rolls. Engaging professional auditors, accountants, or nationally certified management professionals can ensure accuracy. Still, the most valuable item to any sponsorship group is a due diligence checklist.

Protecting the Planet

The last phase, environmental due diligence, will be discussed here. It involves assessing the property to identify any environmental hazards and check compliance with environmental regulations. A thorough environmental due diligence process helps investors mitigate risks linked with contamination, natural disasters, and regulatory compliance.

The process usually begins with a Phase I Environmental Site Assessment (ESA), which involves investigating the historical uses of the property and adjacent sites to determine potential sources of contamination. The property is inspected to detect any signs of environmental hazards, such as storage tanks, chemical spills, or illegal dumping. Additionally, a thorough review of federal, state, and local ecological records is performed to uncover any reported environmental issues or regulatory violations. Interviews with current and past property owners, occupants, and local authorities are also conducted to gather further information on potential environmental concerns.

A Phase II ESA may be needed if the Phase I Environmental Site Assessment (ESA) identifies potential environmental hazards. This phase involves collecting soil, water, and air samples for laboratory testing to confirm the presence and extent of contamination. The risks tied to any identified contamination are then evaluated, including potential health impacts and remediation costs.

In addition to ESAs, in some cases, Environmental Impact Assessments (EIAs) are conducted to assess the potential environmental impacts of planned developments or renovations on the property and surrounding areas. Strategies are developed to mitigate identified ecological consequences, such as erosion control, noise reduction, and habitat preservation. Public involvement is also significant, where the local community and stakeholders are engaged to collect input and address any concerns related to the project's environmental impact.

A natural disaster risk assessment is another component of environmental due diligence. This assessment evaluates the property's risk of natural disasters, including flood risk, by reviewing floodplain maps and historical flood data, earthquake risk by assessing seismic hazard maps and building codes, and the potential for other natural disasters such as hurricanes, tornadoes, and wildfires. The property's preparedness and resilience to these disasters are thoroughly examined.

To ensure compliance and verifiable data, engage experienced environmental consultants to conduct thorough assessments and provide expert guidance on remediation and compliance, if necessary, on your chosen asset. Use Geographic Information Systems (GIS) tools to analyze environmental data, such as floodplains, seismic hazard maps, and land use records. As a final tool, federal, state, and local environmental databases can be used to gather information on historical and current ecological conditions and compliance requirements.

The Ultimate DD Guide

This Due Diligence Checklist covers the critical aspects of financial, legal, physical, and environmental assessments needed for acquiring a multifamily property. The list may not be all-encompassing, and as you move through multiple transactions, additional items will be required (e.g., elevators). Not all the specified items will be available from the seller.

Financial Due Diligence

Review of Financial Statements

1. Income Statements—Three Years and Year to Date (YTD).
2. General Ledger / Balance Sheets—One Year and Year to Date (YTD).
3. Cash Flow Statements—Three Years and Year to Date (YTD).
4. Operating Account Bank Statements—One Year and Year to Date (YTD).

Rent Roll Analysis

1. Current Rent Roll—Updated for the lease audit and unit walk.
2. Historical and Current Occupancy—One Year and Year to Date (YTD).
3. Delinquency Report—One Year and Year to Date (YTD).
4. Copy of current rental rates, security deposits, and move-in specials offered.

5. Itemization of existing reoccurring rent concessions, if any. Or acknowledgment that none exists.

6. List of all Section 8 housing or subsidized residents. Identify both the resident and the related housing authority, if any. Or acknowledgment that none exists.

Expense Verification

1. Utility Bills (water, sewer, electric, and gas for individual units paid by the landlord and any amenity space)—One Year and Year to Date (YTD).

2. You will also need to have:

    a. Trash invoices: Last three months.

    b. Itemized capital expenditures:—Five Years and Year to Date (YTD).

    c. Current Payroll: List the employee, job duty, weekly hours worked, pay rate, and employee rent concessions, if applicable.

    d. Advertising invoices: Three months.

    e. Current marketing brochures and materials.

Debt Review

1. Copy of the latest mortgage invoice.

Tax Records

1. Copy of all Property Tax Bills for all parcels—Two Years.
2. Copy of all Property Tax Payments for all parcels—Two Years.
3. Check for outstanding tax liens.

Vendor Contracts and Agreements

1. Copy of all existing vendor contracts. Delineate those that are intended to survive closing. Or acknowledgment that none exists.
2. Copy of Cable TV or Internet revenue sharing agreement. Or acknowledgment that none exists.
3. Copy of Laundry Rental Lease, if applicable. Or acknowledgment that none exists.

Legal Due Diligence

Title Review

1. Obtain a title report for the property.

2. Secure title insurance based on the title report.

Lease Agreements

Copy of a blank lease, addendums, application, and other move-in paperwork.

Zoning and Land Use

All written city correspondence about code violations or complaints, if any. Or acknowledgment that none exists (two years).

- Environmental regulations.
- Copy of any previously completed Phase I or Phase II.
- Litigation and disputes.
- Contact information of the Attorney who performs resident evictions.
- Copy of any pending litigation related to the property or entity—Two Years.
- Review any dispute resolution mechanisms.
- Insurance policies: Insurance Loss Runs (or written acknowledgment of no known claims)—Five Years.

Physical Due Diligence

- Property inspections and condition assessments.
- The exact address of each building is listed on a site map.
- Personal Property Inventory to be sold with the property.
- Copy of the most recent survey.
- Copy of the most recent existing appraisal and site inspection/assessment report.

Mechanical Systems

1. Copies of any HVAC upgrades or replacement invoices—Three Years.
2. Copies of any major plumbing upgrades or replacement invoices—Three Years.
3. Copies of any significant electrical upgrades or replacements invoices—Three Years.
4. Copies of roof repair or replacement invoices—Three Years.

Safety and Compliance

1. Copies of any fire safety inspections, repairs, or replacements—Three Years.
2. Copies of any security systems inspections, repairs, or replacements—Three Years.

Environmental Due Diligence

Phase I ESA

- Copy of any previously completed Phase I.

Phase II ESA (If Needed)

- Copy of any previously completed Phase II, if applicable. Or acknowledgment that none exists.

Environmental Impact Assessments (EIA)

- Copy of any previously completed EIA, if applicable. Or acknowledgment that none exists.

Natural Disaster Risk Assessment

- Copies of any emergency or natural disaster occurrences—Three Years.

Due Diligence in Action

Case Study – Physical Insights Unveiled

For this Subject Property, a detailed physical due diligence process was conducted to identify any issues and plan for necessary improvements:

Inspection Process

- Exterior and common areas: The inspection revealed minor cracks in the foundation, which required immediate attention. Landscaping was well-maintained, but parking lot resurfacing was needed.
- Mechanical systems: HVAC systems were found to be outdated and inefficient, prompting a plan for replacement. Plumbing inspections uncovered minor leaks that were repaired promptly. Electrical systems were up to code but required new circuit breakers.
- Safety and compliance: Fire safety systems were functional but needed updating to meet the latest standards. Security systems were adequate but enhanced with additional cameras and improved lighting.

Key Findings

- Necessary plumbing and HVAC repairs were identified.
- Cosmetic updates, such as painting and carpeting in common areas, were planned to improve aesthetics.

- Immediate structural repairs to address foundation cracks were prioritized.

Implications

- The findings impacted the renovation budget and timeline, requiring adjustments to the initial financial projections.
- A comprehensive renovation plan was developed to address both immediate repairs and long-term improvements.

Case Study: Unit Walk Discoveries

Common Issues

- Leaking faucets, non-compliant GFCI outlets, and worn-out flooring were common issues across multiple units.

Prioritization

- Immediate repairs were prioritized to prevent further damage and ensure tenant safety.

Renovation Schedule

- Units were scheduled for upgrades in phases to minimize disruption to current tenants. This included upgrading kitchens and bathrooms, repainting, and replacing old flooring. Premium upgrades included full renovations.

Case Study: Unpacking Legal Layers

For the Subject Property, a comprehensive legal due diligence process was conducted to identify any potential legal issues and ensure compliance with all regulations:

Title Review

- Title report: The title report confirmed clear ownership of the property but identified an easement that required further investigation.
- Title insurance: Title insurance was secured to protect against future claims.

Lease Agreements

- Current leases: All existing lease agreements were reviewed. Some leases had clauses that required renegotiation to align with the new management's policies.
- Tenant rights: The leases were compliant with local tenant laws, and no major issues were found.

Zoning and Land Use

- Zoning compliance: The property was found to be in compliance with current zoning laws. Additionally, future development plans in the area were noted, which could potentially increase the property's value.

Environmental Regulations

- Environmental assessments: Phase I ESA identified no significant issues thus a Phase II ESA was not necessary.

- Compliance: The property was compliant with all environmental regulations.

Litigation and Disputes

- Pending litigation: There were no pending lawsuits or regulatory investigations involving the property.
- Dispute resolution: Existing dispute resolution mechanisms in the contracts were deemed adequate.

Vendor Contracts

- Service agreements: Reviewed all vendor contracts. Most contracts had clear termination clauses, allowing for easy transition to new service providers if needed.
- Termination clauses: Ensured that all contracts included termination clauses favorable to the new management.

Insurance Policies

- Current coverage: Existing insurance policies provided adequate coverage, but additional coverage for specific risks was recommended.

Case Study: Financial Truths Revealed

For Subject Property, a detailed financial due diligence process was conducted to verify the property's financial health and identify any discrepancies:

Review of Financial Statements

- Income statements: The income statements were analyzed, revealing steady revenue streams and identifying areas for potential income growth through rent increases and improved occupancy.

A clear difference in potential market rent and the current rent intake can be seen in the examples listed below:

- Balance sheets: The balance sheets showed a healthy balance of assets and liabilities, with sufficient equity to support future investments.
- Cash flow statements: Cash flow statements indicated strong liquidity but suggested opportunities for better cash flow management.

Rent Roll Analysis

- Current Rent Roll: The Rent Roll was verified against lease agreements, confirming the accuracy of tenant information and rental rates.
- Occupancy rates: Historical occupancy rates were analyzed, showing consistent demand and low vacancies.
- Rent collection: Rent collection records indicated high collection efficiency, with minimal issues related to delinquent tenants.

Property Current Effective Rent

Unit	Rent	Rent PSF	Rent Monthly	Rent Annualized
1bd/1ba Upstairs Classic	$664	$1.11	$26,560	$318,720
1bd/1ba Down Classic	$684	$1.14	$27,360	$328,320
2bd/1ba Upstairs Classic	$780	$1.04	$29,640	$355,680
2ba/1ba Down Classic	$800	$1.07	$30,400	$364,800
1bd/1ba Upstairs Upgraded	$0	$0.00	$0	$0
1bd/1ba Down Upgraded	$0	$0.00	$0	$0
2bd/1ba Upstairs Upgraded	$0	$0.00	$0	$0
2ba/1ba Down Upgraded	$0	$0.00	$0	$0
1bd/1ba Upstairs Premium	$0	$0.00	$0	$0
1bd/1ba Down Premium	$0	$0.00	$0	$0
2bd/1ba Upstairs Premium	$0	$0.00	$0	$0
2ba/1ba Down Premium	$0	$0.00	$0	$0
	731	**1.09**	**$113,960**	**$1,367,520**

Property Market Rents

# of Units	Rent	Rent PSF	Rent Monthly	Rent Annualized
12	$815	$1.36	$9,780	$117,360
12	$830	$1.38	$9,960	$119,520
11	$935	$1.25	$10,659	$127,908
11	$950	$1.27	$10,830	$129,960
20	$815	$1.36	$16,300	$195,600
20	$830	$1.38	$16,600	$199,200
19	$935	$1.25	$17,765	$213,180
19	$950	$1.27	$18,050	$216,600
8	$815	$1.36	$6,520	$78,240
8	$830	$1.38	$6,640	$79,680
8	$935	$1.25	$7,106	$85,272
8	$950	$1.27	$7,220	$86,640
156	**881**	**1.31**	**$137,430**	**$1,649,160**

Expense Verification

- Operating expenses: Operating expenses were validated through invoices and payment records, maintaining accuracy and identifying areas for cost savings.
- Maintenance and repairs: Maintenance records revealed consistent upkeep but also highlighted the need for future capital expenditures.
- Capital expenditures: Records of past capital expenditures were reviewed, confirming investments in property improvements and identifying planned future projects.

Tax Records

- Property tax assessments: Property tax assessments and payments were reviewed for their accuracy and to identify any discrepancies.
- Tax liens: No outstanding tax liens were found, confirming the property's clear financial standing.

Vendor Contracts and Agreements

- Service contracts: Contracts with service providers were examined, ensuring they were favorable and aligned with the property's operational needs.
- Lease agreements: Lease agreements were consistent and complied with local regulations, providing a stable legal foundation for the property's operations.

Natural Disaster Risk Assessment

- Flood risk: The property was located outside the 100-year floodplain, minimizing flood risk.
- Earthquake risk: The property was assessed for seismic vulnerability, and it was determined that the buildings met current earthquake-resistant building codes.
- Other natural disasters: No significant risks from other natural disasters were identified.

Environmental:

- Permits and approvals: All necessary environmental permits were reviewed and found to be in order.
- Compliance history: The property's compliance history was examined, revealing no major violations or enforcement actions.

Building the Vision

When it comes to construction work, you have a few different options to consider. One approach is to hire a general contractor. In this case, it's wise to reach out to at least three contractors for bids on both labor and materials. Make sure they break down the costs so you can see exactly what you're paying for. Depending on the scale of your portfolio, you might have better material purchasing power than they do, so keep that in mind. Assess the labor costs alongside the estimated time it will take to complete the work.

Alternatively, you could use your in-house maintenance staff. If you have a dedicated construction team that moves between locations, this can be a cost-effective choice. Another option is to hire a construction manager who can solicit bids from subcontractors for each specific task, whether it's roofing, painting, or plumbing. A construction manager essentially acts as a general contractor on behalf of the property owner.

Keep in mind that certain skilled labor—like electrical or plumbing work—might be beyond the scope of your maintenance technicians, and you may need to bring in licensed professionals. Structural design work will also require the expertise of a licensed architect. Ultimately, you want to determine the most cost-effective and efficient way to achieve your renovation goals.

Using a contractor has its benefits, such as having a single point of contact, but it does not mean relying on a third party to bring your vision to life. It can limit your control over the outcome. Additionally, friction can sometimes arise between contractors and engineers or architects. Contractors often focus on value engineering, which might not always align with your project goals. Typically, they provide a lump-sum bid at the beginning of the project, including a small contingency.

On the flip side, handling construction in-house may mean juggling multiple contractors, but it gives you more control over both the design and construction processes. With this approach, you can make adjustments on the fly, potentially lowering costs and improving efficiency. A construction manager incentivized to reduce costs for ownership can also help maintain control over the schedule and cash flow, providing you with valuable insights during the design phase.

When selecting a contractor, it's crucial to evaluate each one thoroughly. Obtain at least three bids and verify their reputations, track records, availability, and workforce size. Local contractors can offer distinct advantages; they understand the market and can respond quickly if issues arise. Plus, supporting local businesses stimulates the economy.

I remember a time when I managed a 342-unit property in Indiana. A gentleman approached me wanting to start an HVAC business after receiving his certification. He proposed competitive pricing, around 40% lower than our regional contractor. I agreed to give him a chance under one condition: he had to respond to our maintenance team's calls for HVAC issues 24/7. He delivered on that promise, building a successful company that now serves the region today.

When evaluating your options for construction work, it's beneficial to weigh the pros and cons of each approach based on your specific project needs, budget, and timeline. A general contractor offers a streamlined process since they oversee the entire project from start to finish. By requesting detailed bids from multiple contractors, you create transparency in cost breakdowns, which can reveal opportunities for savings- particularly if you're able to source materials at a lower price than what the contractor proposes. This can be especially advantageous if your project involves significant material costs, where your purchasing power could make a difference in the overall budget.

On the other hand, utilizing an in-house maintenance or construction team is a hands-on approach that can potentially reduce expenses and grant you more control over scheduling and execution. If you already have a mobile team skilled in basic construction tasks, this can be an ideal solution for smaller or ongoing projects across multiple locations. The in-house team approach can also facilitate quicker responses to unexpected issues or changes in project scope since there's no need to renegotiate with an outside contractor over a change order.

In cases where specialized work is required, such as plumbing, electrical, or structural renovations, it's advised to bring in licensed professionals. Not only does this ensure compliance with local building codes, but it also protects the safety and structural integrity of the property. While subcontracting these trades can slightly increase the project cost, the investment is justified by the high quality and longevity of the work completed. A construction manager can assist here by coordinating bids from multiple subcontractors, allowing you to compare rates and credentials for each specific task.

Opting for a construction manager rather than a general contractor may be particularly effective if your renovation is complex or requires precision in scheduling and budget management. This approach allows you to oversee each phase of the project, enhancing both cost-effectiveness and quality control, but often sacrificing time. Additionally, construction managers can liaise with architects or engineers so that the project design aligns with your vision and is executed within budget constraints. By breaking down the work into specific contracts, the manager can keep a close eye on costs, timing, and quality without the additional markup that a general contractor might apply to subcontractor services.

For larger projects, contractor selection becomes especially important. When assessing bids, prioritize contractors with a proven history of delivering on time and within budget. Requesting references and speaking with former clients can offer valuable insights into the contractor's professionalism, responsiveness, and adaptability under pressure. A reputable local contractor not only brings knowledge of the local market but can also provide quick response times in the event of unforeseen issues. This proximity can be an asset, especially for maintenance work that requires immediate attention.

Reflecting on past experiences, like the one in Indiana, highlights the value of partnerships with emerging local contractors who may offer competitive rates and flexible service terms. In this instance, entrusting the HVAC work to a newly certified contractor resulted in both cost savings and long-term service reliability. By setting clear expectations, such as requiring 24/7 availability for maintenance calls, the property management secured a dependable service provider while supporting a local entrepreneur's growth. In comparison, In Michigan, on a 312-unit property, we decided to paint the building exteriors after receiving three bids. The cheaper local contractor was chosen, and he ran off with the deposits. This is why we require three references for all new vendors.

Once bids are collected, evaluate each contractor based not only on price but also on the quality of their past work and their reputation. Engaging former clients in conversations about the contractor's adherence to schedules, ability to handle challenges, and the quality of their craftsmanship can help ensure you make an informed decision.

A general list of items to include in a bid:

Kitchen

- Cabinet removal
- Install new cabinets
- Install countertops
- Install vinyl plank
- Clean exhaust fans

- Installed kitchen sink
- Replace faucet with sprayer
- Replace angle valves
- Replace fixtures with LED

Bathroom

- Replace all valves
- Replace wax ring
- Replace toilet low flow
- Install medicine cabinet
- Replace light fixtures with LED
- Replace faucet bath
- Replace the faucet sink
- Clean exhaust fan and other interior work

Painting

- Cleaning with carpet shampoo
- Cleaning without carpet shampoo
- Removing carpet
- Secure subfloor
- Installing mini blinds
- Installing thresholds
- Installing solid core doors
- Install hollow core doors
- Replace doorstops
- Change air conditioning filters
- Change thermostat
- Install peep holes
- Replace light switch plates

- Replace outlets

Replace light switches, don't cover them. Don't be cheap—it will bite you later. The resident will hate it. Renewals will drop.

Streamlining Construction

The Critical Path Method (CPM) is a scheduling tool widely used in construction project management to determine the most efficient timeline for completing tasks. It identifies specific activities, their sequence, and the time each task requires. Essentially, the method highlights the critical path, which is the sequence of tasks that dictates the minimum duration necessary to complete the project.

Let us look at the example below. Tasks 1, 2, 3, and 4, plus tasks 5 and 6 are part of two separate series of activities in a repositioning project. Since tasks 5 and 6 take a total of 5 days, they form the critical path, which becomes the longest sequence of dependent activities that determine the project's duration. Task 7, which can only start after the completion of both series, will add 2 more days, bringing the critical path's total to 7 days.

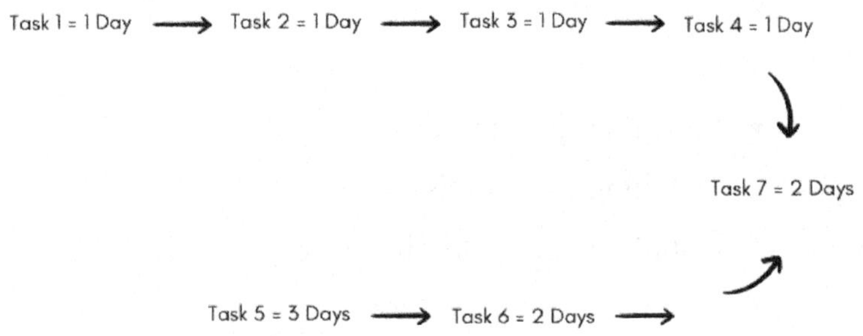

For complex repositioning, CPM is crucial because it not only sets a realistic timeline for completion but also helps project managers identify areas where delays may occur. Furthermore, it allows for more efficient resource allocation and ensures that all concurrent activities and dependencies are accounted for in scheduling.

When preparing bids for renovation projects, there are numerous budget components to consider. Here's a comprehensive list to guide you, though it may not be exhaustive:

- **Permits:** Always factor in the costs associated with obtaining necessary permits.
- **Electrical:** This includes repairs and upgrades, such as moving from a 60-amp to a 125-amp service. You may also need to pull new wiring from the street if the existing service can't support appliances like washers and dryers. Don't forget to include the installation of new wiring in walls, as well as replacements for ceiling light fixtures, wall switches, and outlets.
- **Plumbing:** Budget for underground pipe repairs or replacements, connections within walls, along with fixtures such as faucets, sinks, basins, bathtubs, and toilets. Replacing valves will reward you in the long term. Be proactive about water heaters.
- **Elevator:** Consider costs for repair or replacement and ongoing service contracts.
- **Heating systems:** This includes the repair or replacement of furnaces, air conditioning units, and boilers.
- **Foundation:** Any necessary foundation work should be included in your budget.
- **Roof:** Determine if repairs or a complete replacement is needed.
- **Painting:** Account for both interior and exterior painting costs.

- **Windows:** Budget for repairs or replacements.
- **Appliances:** When replacing appliances, try to keep sets uniform. It's important to avoid mismatched appliances, like a black dishwasher next to a white stove; the aesthetic difference can be minimal, sometimes just $20, but it is exponential to buyers and residents.
- **Cabinets:** Consider whether to repair or replace cabinets. Painting existing cabinets or replacing only doors and drawers can give a fresh look while remaining cost-effective. However, double-check that the cabinet boxes are solid; if they're damaged or made of particle board, they'll likely need replacement.
- **Carpeting:** I recommend using carpet only in bedrooms and opting for vinyl composite tile (VCT) in common areas. Using 8mm for interiors and 12mm for high-traffic areas will help manage long-term replacement costs.
- **Window coverings:** Install new, uniform window coverings. When residents damage these, replace them with a consistent style.
- **Labor:** Include costs for all labor involved in the project.
- **Landscaping:** Don't forget to budget for any necessary landscaping work or irrigation.
- **Parking lot:** Consider costs for repair or replacement.
- **Contingency:** Always set aside a contin-

gency budget for unexpected expenses, usually 10% of the budget.

This detailed approach will help ensure that your bids are comprehensive and that you've accounted for all potential costs.

Using the Critical Path Method (CPM) in construction management provides a clear roadmap for project completion, especially in multifaceted repositioning projects where various tasks depend on each other. The CPM pinpoints which activities are critical to avoid delays and keeps the project on track. In our example, tasks 5 and 6 make up the critical path due to their combined 5-day duration, with task 7 extending the total project timeline to 7 days. By recognizing this sequence, project managers can plan and allocate resources more effectively, minimizing downtime.

In addition to scheduling, developing a comprehensive and realistic budget is needed. Permits are often overlooked but can contribute significantly to project costs. For major renovation work, like electrical upgrades, planning is critical. Shifting from a 60-amp to a 125-amp service requires rewiring, which may necessitate new cables from external sources, along with updates for internal fixtures like outlets and switches. Plumbing, too, can be costly if pipes are deteriorating or if fixtures need upgrades. Budgeting for repairs or replacements of faucets, toilets, and pipes within walls can prevent unexpected issues down the line.

Elevator systems and heating systems are other major budget items, especially for older buildings where replacements or upgrades may be necessary to meet new safety standards. Any foundation work should also be included, as this can impact the structural integrity of the entire building. Roof work is a high priority in many repositioning projects, as delays in repairs or replacement can lead to more extensive damage.

Aesthetic aspects, while sometimes viewed as secondary,

significantly impact the property's appeal. Painting, both interior and exterior, should be budgeted to refresh the property's look. Similarly, maintaining uniformity with appliances is critical. Appliances should be of a similar make and color to avoid aesthetic inconsistencies that could affect tenant satisfaction and even rentability. Cabinets can also be an important feature—consider repairing and repainting existing ones if they're structurally sound, as this may be more cost-effective than a complete replacement.

Flooring choices impact both aesthetic and practical aspects of the property. Using carpets only in bedrooms and opting for more durable materials like VCT in high-traffic areas can reduce long-term maintenance costs. Selecting the right thickness (e.g., 8 mm for apartments and 12 mm for high-traffic spaces) can further extend the floor's lifespan. Deep cleaning can be more economical than carpet replacements, so planning for periodic replacements can be part of a cost-saving approach.

Window coverings, while a small detail, contribute to the uniformity and professional look of a unit. Consistency in style across units creates a cohesive look and simplifies replacements. Including a contingency budget is essential to handle unforeseen circumstances without compromising project quality.

Debt and Lending Essentials

Financing a property repositioning can be challenging due to market conditions, limited financing options, and the risks involved. Typically, lenders base loans on pro forma financials, projections of the property's performance after renovations, making repositioning loans among the hardest to secure. They carry high risks because if projected targets aren't met, the borrower risks losing the asset and investment. The cyclical nature of real estate adds complexity as the types of financing and construction methods available evolve with market conditions. Yet, once a project begins, it's nearly impossible to halt, even if market shifts would otherwise suggest stopping. After securing financing, the repositioning must proceed to increase the value as projected to have any hope of yielding a profit for the sponsor and meeting the lender requirements.

Repositioning success depends heavily on rigorous transaction analysis centered purely on economic viability. In real estate, due diligence is critical. With sound analysis and an economically viable property, finding a lender becomes possible. However, lenders prefer borrowers with equity and capital at stake, a strong track record, and financial stability. Below is a list of documents commonly required for a loan application:

1. Loan application.
2. Executed LLC-related documents.
3. Schedule of real estate investments, including cash flow, income, expenses, loan balances, and lender information for each investment.
4. Recent financial statements of principals (within

the last 90 days) and income tax returns for the past three years for both borrowers and principals.

5. Verification of deposits for all bank accounts.
6. Personal and/or professional credit references.
7. Previous track record (if applicable).
8. Lender-ordered credit report.
9. Property operating statement for the past 3 years, the current year-to-date, and a pro forma for the upcoming year for the subject property.
10. Certified Rent Roll (often inspected by the buyer, with no third-party verification; inflating this can result in fraud if not properly checked).
11. Delinquency report listing tenants who are over 30 days past due with rents exceeding $200.
12. Occupancy history for the subject property over the past 12 months.
13. Management plan for the property or confirmation of the management company's track record.
14. Copy of the management agreement detailing terms and compensation.
15. Validly executed lease copies.
16. Vendor contracts.
17. List of site personnel and their resumes.
18. Certificate of occupancy.
19. Current property insurance policy and proof of payment.

20. Real estate, tax, water, and sewer bills for the past 3 years.

21. Utility bills for the past 3 years.

22. Tax account number and jurisdiction for the property.

23. Title insurance for the property.

24. Survey showing all easements on the subject property.

25. Aerial photography of the property.

26. Scheduled improvements.

27. List of professional services used by the borrower (attorney, accountant, etc.).

For renovation dollars, lenders will likely require multiple construction draws overseen by a construction manager. These must include inspection reports, check requests, payment applications, sworn statements, lien waivers (conditional and unconditional), and other supporting documents. This way, the funds are properly allocated and accounted for during the repositioning process.

As we conclude the chapter on due diligence, it's important to recognize that this phase is one of the most critical in any real estate transaction. Proper due diligence ensures that you are not only buying the property for the right price but also protecting yourself from hidden liabilities and potential pitfalls. Skipping or rushing through this stage can lead to significant financial losses, unforeseen legal complications, and long-term operational challenges.

Due diligence is your opportunity to gather all the information you need to make an informed decision. From reviewing title documents and zoning laws to inspecting the physical condition of the property, each aspect of this process plays a vital role in determining whether the investment is sound. The financial health of the property, its occupancy history, the surrounding market, and even the management team should all be thoroughly evaluated to mitigate risks.

It's also necessary to work with qualified professionals during due diligence; attorneys, inspectors, appraisers, and property managers can offer critical insights that might otherwise be overlooked. The more thorough your due diligence, the better positioned you'll be to negotiate terms that benefit you and protect your investment.

In real estate, knowledge is power, and due diligence is where you arm yourself with the information needed to succeed. With due diligence completed, we now shift focus to another component of real estate success: operations. Understanding how to effectively manage and operate a property helps your investment continue to grow in value.

Once the deal is closed and due diligence is behind you, the focus shifts to the day-to-day operations of the property. Operations are the engine that keeps your investment running smoothly so that tenants are happy, expenses are managed, and the property maintains or increases its value over time. Effective operations are not just about collecting rent—they involve everything from maintenance and repairs to managing tenant relationships and maintaining compliance with local laws.

In this chapter, we'll explore the foundational principles of property operations, the key roles involved, and the strategies successful operators use to maximize returns. Whether you're managing the property yourself or working with a management company, understanding the essentials of property operations is crucial to long-term profitability.

CHAPTER 4

Mastering Property Operations

Operating a multifamily asset is like adjusting a cruise boat. It only takes a few minor adjustments to stay on course. However, being one degree off, overtime, will eventually be significantly off course.

What do you think when I say the word operations? Do you think of operations as the intricate machinery that keeps a multifamily property running smoothly, from leasing and tenant relations to maintenance and financial reporting?

Just as a well-oiled machine needs regular upkeep and fine-tuning, effective property operations demand continuous attention and adaptation to meet evolving tenant needs and market dynamics.

As we delve into this chapter, we'll explore the fundamental components of multifamily operations, emphasizing the importance of a proactive management approach. You will learn how operational strategies not only enhance tenant satisfaction but also drive revenue and increase asset value. We'll cover essential topics, including lease management, occupancy strategies, and maintenance protocols, highlighting how each plays a pivotal role in long-term success.

Frankly, this is the point in the transaction's lifetime

when the sponsors have the least experience, and it is the most critical part of the process. They often have no policy or prior procedural knowledge to fix a distressed asset. Sponsors frequently hire third-party management with the goal of relentless expansion. The lack of attention to operations by asset managers is staggering for such a meaningful aspect of the multifamily transaction.

Property management encompasses all activities related to the day-to-day running of the property. Effective operations management ensures that the property remains in good condition, tenants are satisfied, and the financial performance of the investment is optimized. I would also propose that professional and efficient property management increases intangible value, generally allowing the operator to command a premium for their efforts from both ownership and tenants.

A property transformation is not only physical; it is equally a social adjustment of a distressed property within an individual market. Changing a culture through property operations is the intangible that plagues this industry. Changing the perception of a distressed and depreciated property can take months, if not years, to accomplish, while the physical transformation can happen quickly.

In their haste, value-added sponsors often only focus on the physical aspect of the property in the hope that their operations team can make up for the difference. Transitioning from the current resident profile to the projected resident profile can take time and requires the reposition of any distressed asset.

Your residents are your best and can be your worst advertising. Once someone has chosen your property, consideration for their needs is paramount. Inexperienced or unsupervised management can cause a property to decline, leading to frustrated staff, increased vacancies, increased work order timelines, and increased marketing expenses. This devolution of an asset takes time—not a week, not even months. At times, it takes up to a year or two. Deferred maintenance leads to tenant dissatisfaction, causing additional turnover.

As management becomes more distant, the residents will begin defining the rules and policies. Frequently, the surrounding neighborhood can see signs of decline before ownership, amplifying the gossip and reputation mill. Create a soft, welcoming entrance and curb appeal to set a firm foundation with the residents and community that a change is coming. Continue with your other exterior renovations that have been planned, including landscaping, asphalt repair or replacement, building exteriors, and other lender-required repairs, and define the path forward for the culture of your property.

There are two types of renters. Renters by necessity, who cannot afford a home. Then, there are renters by choice, who frequently make a decision based on amenities, location, or luxury instead of primarily focusing on price. Developers have recently combined these by creating Single-Family for Rent (SFR) communities, allowing renters to avoid a shared wall at a comparable price point. I am concerned about these assets' long-term deferred maintenance for underwriting and future repositioning conversations.

Property management is a detail-oriented business. From your first asset tour, you should evaluate the current management, deferred maintenance, physical condition, and neighborhood. The staff's dress and attitude can tell you more than their words. Are they professional?

While onsite staff knowledge is usually irreplaceable, your business plan may call for the termination of all current staff, but they know where the bodies are buried. Please get to know them; a leadership or procedural problem may have caused the issue. Often, they are terrified for their job, and when they feel grilled for lack of occupancy or a drop in collections, a property manager will shut down.

Take notes from day one about their appearance, professionalism, attitude, and salary. This will allow you to recall details later when compiling your data. I always ask a manager for the top three resident complaints, top three work order calls, favorite part of the property, what would you fix with a $1M budget. Don't forget to get the existing managers' opinion on staff turnover. Each question provides me with critical information about how the property is managed and the residents' perceptions.

Operational management is the most crucial role in the success of any multifamily property. One of the primary aspects of effective operations is tenant satisfaction. By offering responsive maintenance and maintaining open, effective communication, onsite staff can ensure a high level of tenant satisfaction, leading to longer lease terms and lower vacancy rates. Additionally, operations are a pivotal component of enhancing the property's value. Regular maintenance and strategic upgrades keep the property in good condition and competitive within the market. Optimizing operational efficiency helps control costs and maximize profits; transparently, it's just easier to run a property that is running efficiently.

In the following sections, we will explore multiple components of multifamily operations, beginning with the preparation for property takeovers. Preparing for a smooth transition is critical to maintaining stability for the property and the residents. Once this foundation is set, we will delve into property management, which encompasses the daily operations that keep the property running smoothly and efficiently.

Tenant relations are another basic aspect, as managing tenant interactions and fostering a sense of community can significantly impact occupancy rates and resident satisfaction. The following section will cover maintenance and repairs, focusing on the importance of regular upkeep to prevent more significant, costly issues so the property remains in top condition.

We will also discuss expense management, which is needed for keeping the property within budget while maximizing profitability. Finally, we will briefly touch on the role of technology in modern property management, exploring how advancements in software and systems can streamline operations and improve overall efficiency.

By focusing on these components, property managers can make sure that the multifamily property operates efficiently, enhances tenant satisfaction, and achieves financial success. The following sections will provide detailed insights and strategies for effectively managing each of these areas.

Smooth Transition Strategies

You are finally prepared to close. All the documents are signed, and the funds are in escrow. You are waiting to hear from the title company that you are the new owner. Sometimes, the first half of the day is wasted waiting for the property to be recorded by the title company. I would encourage you to take this time to become intimately knowledgeable about the asset.

Transitioning a property takes a monumental effort with a team of people. Ensuring a smooth transition and uninterrupted operations is an undervalued skill. This process involves detailed planning and coordination with staff, tenants, and vendors to minimize disruptions and maintain tenant satisfaction.

A well-organized transition plan is a must-have for a seamless takeover. Effective communication with all stakeholders, beginning with tenants, is key. A detailed communication plan that includes letters, meetings, and newsletters for informing them about the change in ownership or management. These efforts help address any concerns and outline the benefits of the new management.

Additionally, communication with existing staff is crucial. Their concerns should be addressed, their roles clarified, and any necessary training on new processes or systems provided. Existing vendors must also be notified about the change, and the remaining contracts from Due Diligence will be in full effect.

Operational setup is another vital aspect of the takeover process. Setting up property management software will streamline your operations by managing tenant information and handling maintenance requests. New bank accounts and financial management systems should be established for rent collection, expenses, and reporting. The new management must also transfer utility accounts and service contracts for uninterrupted services. Generally, this is completed by the management chosen by the sponsorship group.

Staffing and training are integral to maintaining efficient operations post-takeover. Evaluating the current staffing levels will help determine if additional staff are needed, and new hires should be promptly onboarded and trained. Implementing training programs for new and existing staff creates familiarity with the property's operations, management software, and tenant relations practices, helping them provide high-quality service to tenants.

I prefer one office member and one maintenance member per 100 units, plus or minus 25 units based on age. The newer the property, the less maintenance you may need. Perhaps, your site requires more administrative work, and you may need more staff. In general, the economy of scale triggers around 80 units.

Finally, maintenance and repairs must be addressed early in the process. You will probably have a backlog of maintenance requests stuffed in desks, in the shop, or in the trash. Be prepared for a flood of calls from residents with requests and be ready to handle them quickly. Once the backlog has been resolved over the first few weeks, you should strive to maintain a 72-hour work order policy and 24-hour emergency maintenance.

Managing for Success

The takeover of a multifamily property requires meticulous planning and coordination for a smooth transition. While professional management is needed in operating any multifamily asset, its importance grows significantly during the repositioning and renovation phases. During these periods, management becomes far more intensive as the property undergoes rapid changes, requiring the operations team to keep the situation as stable as possible. Essentially, this phase often becomes a form of crisis management, with the site manager playing a pivotal role in day-to-day property oversight and construction management. The management of staff, coordination of policies and procedures, and alignment with marketing efforts must all work in harmony with the reposition process to ensure the project's successful conclusion.

Property management is an incredibly detail-oriented business in these situations, demanding that managers remain adaptable to the constant changes occurring on-site. The site manager must possess strong leadership qualities to direct staff and foster a cooperative atmosphere, especially during times of transition. Balancing the dual role of enforcing the owner's goals while providing quality service to residents is challenging but necessary. A manager must be firm in enforcing property rules while being approachable and optimistic, maintaining an upbeat attitude that reflects a forward-moving and proactive marketing effort.

Managing a stable property is vastly different from managing one undergoing renovation. While the duties and responsibilities are basically the same, the challenges of renovation introduce a new layer of complexity. Changes will be frequent, and both residents and staff may find them distressing. The site manager must remain steady, providing a sense of consistency amid the chaos. The experience and capability of the management team during this period can significantly impact the project's ultimate success.

One of the first tasks in taking over a property, especially one slated for renovation, is thoroughly reviewing its current management structure and operations. During the due diligence process, you should have already gained some insight into potential issues with how the property was managed previously. However, once the property is officially under your control, a more detailed assessment is necessary to inform you of the changes and improvements you plan to implement. This deeper dive will serve as the foundation for transforming the property and setting it on a new path toward success.

Regardless of the occupancy level or the overall quality of the existing residents, the property is in trouble—a factor that was likely considered in your search for a property to reposition. This negative situation has sent a strong message to the residents, who have acted as they please. Some may be paying rent late or not at all, throwing wild parties, working on cars in the parking lot, intimidating other residents, and engaging in other unacceptable activities. Your immediate priority is to establish order, and the best way to do this is by implementing policies and procedures that provide clear direction for management while signaling to the residents what behaviors *are* and *are not* acceptable. Specific policies and procedures will be discussed later in the chapter.

Another main step is to interview the staff currently employed at the property, including property management personnel and maintenance workers, to clarify their roles and responsibilities. There are two approaches to handling existing staff during a management takeover. One approach is to terminate the entire staff, especially if they have been working without clear rules, leading to bad habits and poor attitudes. In general, termination of a takeover can be a wise decision. Keep in mind that good onsite staff are exceedingly difficult to find.

The other approach is to evaluate each staff member individually and retain those who can work under the new system. It's helpful to recognize that existing staff have one significant advantage over new management; they possess intimate knowledge of the property and its nuances. For instance, long-standing issues, like sewer backups, may be familiar to the current staff, even if they aren't immediately apparent. However, existing staff shouldn't be kept solely because they know the property problems. Instead, they should be assessed like any new candidate, with the same questions and references checked.

Retaining some or all the staff initially can help make the management transition smoother for the residents. At the time of acquisition, the previous staff will likely be demoralized. It's tough for them to come to work daily at a visibly declining property. During the due diligence process, you may find that your plans for repositioning are met with cynicism, regardless of how promising or well-thought-out they may seem. Remember, any property that qualifies for repositioning has likely been evaluated and toured by multiple buyers and mortgage lenders before you. The fact that no previous plans have corrected the property's deficiencies, likely due to limited resources, will only deepen the skepticism among staff who are afraid for their jobs.

It's crucial to be sensitive to their feelings during this time. More information can be gathered if staff members don't feel like they are being interrogated. One-on-one conversations are an excellent opportunity to assess each staff member's abilities. A good question to ask during these evaluations is, "If you were setting the policies for the operations of this property, what would you implement?" Most people work best when clear rules are in place, and policies are consistently enforced. In my experience, some staff members are usually capable of change and willing to follow the rules. Still, they worked in an environment without guidelines and lacked leadership or initiative to find better ways of doing things.

When determining the size of the management staff needed for a multifamily property, the primary consideration will be the site manager and the overall state of the property. The chain of command is key; the site manager must have the authority to select their team, but your guidance should remain a critical factor in the staff selection process. It would help if you interviewed all the staff members yourself. Even though leasing agents may not be immediately necessary during the initial stages of repositioning, you might find that one of the leasing agents can step into the site manager role if the current manager is not suitable. Ultimately, the responsibility of building the management team should be with the site manager you choose.

The individual selected for this role must possess strong leadership qualities that should take precedence over all other traits in the beginning. New policies and procedures must be implemented and enforced, so organizational ability is also compulsory. In our experience, site managers who have operated with minimal oversight tend to develop their own ways of doing things—sometimes, to the detriment of the property. For example, during a lease audit, as part of the due diligence process, you may discover that leases are disorganized or don't align with the Rent Roll. This indicates a lack of organizational skills, a crucial competency for managing a property undergoing repositioning.

The questions you ask while examining the management office will reveal a lot about how the property was previously run and whether the current manager can bring the property up to standard. It's commonly joked in the industry that if everything appears fine, supervisors won't visit the property—there's some truth to this. Site managers tend to feel free to operate in any way they see fit in properties where minimal standards are met. In these cases, extra effort is rarely expended beyond what is necessary to satisfy the owner. Unfortunately, this situation is typical for distressed properties or those taken back by a lender, where ownership is often reluctant to visit due to the property's poor condition, the demoralized staff, or rowdy residents.

During your interview with the existing site manager, you must ask what prior ownership and management expected from them. Communication and interpersonal skills are needed, as the site manager will be your intermediary when interacting with local officials, financial institutions, investors, and others. Although marketing skills may not be as necessary during the initial reposition phase, having a manager with these abilities will be a bonus when the property is ready for leasing. However, in a repositioning scenario, a manager lacking people skills and marketing expertise is unlikely to be an effective leader.

The number of management personnel required will depend on the property size. At the start of a project, you'll typically need at least a manager and an assistant to provide coverage for a six-day workweek. During this period, the management office will not primarily function as a leasing office, but communication alongside policies and procedures must be firmly established. Resident contact will increase, and more thorough property inspections will be necessary.

Keeping residents happy is one of the most vital parts of site management, as the focus will primarily be on rent collection, enforcing policies, and initiating eviction proceedings when necessary. These tasks can be challenging, especially in more significant properties with more than 300 units, where you may need to consider adding a second assistant. There is no hard-and-fast rule for when this becomes necessary; it will depend on the workload of the management team. Sometimes, a part-time assistant may suffice, but minimizing payroll expenses during renovations is important.

Good maintenance staff are hard to find, so interviewing all existing maintenance workers is advisable. It's been said that they are unlikely to change once a maintenance worker develops bad habits, although there have been instances where establishing specific procedures and work rules has led to significantly improved performance. The formal employment interviews you conduct should build on the earlier conversations with the maintenance staff during the due diligence process. When evaluating candidates, don't overlook the importance of people skills. Maintenance personnel interact directly with residents, and their service delivery will influence the opinion of the property.

There is no foolproof method for making the right hiring decision, nor is familiarity with the property always an advantage. For example, a maintenance worker may have worked at the property for years and demonstrated extensive knowledge about the asset and its problems during due diligence. They might have even proposed solutions and expressed enthusiasm for the changes you plan to implement. However, despite talking a good game, this individual may only possess theoretical knowledge. In these cases, it may simply necessitate hiring a replacement. While these decisions may not be costly, they can require several changes before you assemble a team that works well together.

When selecting maintenance personnel for a property undergoing renovation, you need to set specific criteria. Remember that maintenance staff won't be directly involved in the renovation construction work but may occasionally assist with tasks related to renovated units, such as taking delivery of supplies.

It works best if maintenance staff have exclusive access to areas where cabinets, countertops, appliances, and other building materials are stored, often purchased in bulk by the owner. Because of this, the maintenance staff is usually needed to assist in unloading materials as they arrive and delivering them to the units scheduled for use during repositioning. Maintenance staff should also be responsible for the final unit preparation, especially for installing appliances. This ensures that appliances are correctly handled and remain in secure storage until needed.

Similarly, the maintenance team should install or complete items, like window coverings, which are not part of the turnkey construction contract. This also allows maintenance personnel to test all plumbing and electrical systems in the units, just as they would for any vacant unit turnover. Basic tasks, such as tightening loose screws, can be addressed by maintenance staff in a few minutes, saving the contractor a trip back to the unit. While minor issues can be fixed quickly by maintenance, larger oversights or improper installations should be immediately reported to the contractor for correction.

In the past, our maintenance staff was responsible for the initial demolition of units slated for renovation. Over time, though, we found that this became too labor-intensive. Now, tasks like removing carpets, cabinets, flooring, tub enclosures, and light fixtures are included in the contractor's specifications. This approach eliminates overlapping responsibilities and confusion about who is accountable for specific tasks.

Although the maintenance team may participate in the renovations to some extent, their primary responsibility is to provide ongoing services to the property and residents by responding to work orders. When selecting maintenance personnel, choosing individuals with the skills necessary to address the property's specific issues is crucial. For instance, if the property has baseboard heating or uses a low-pressure boiler system, it's essential to have at least one team member with the knowledge to maintain these systems.

Don't forget to delineate responsibilities among the maintenance staff to keep the team as efficient as possible. Maintenance personnel should prioritize responding to work orders from existing residents, handling common area issues, and performing specific tasks in the renovated units. The number of maintenance staff required will depend on various factors, such as the skill level of each worker, the quality and speed of their work, and the number of callbacks they receive. Some workers complete tasks more quickly and accurately than others, which should be considered when determining staffing needs.

Properties undergoing repositioning need to assess recurring maintenance issues and determine whether they should be addressed as part of the renovation. For example, instead of repeatedly sending maintenance staff to clear sewer backups, replacing the sewer lines is a long-term, cost-effective part of the repositioning process. Although this may be a significant upfront expense, it would save money and frustration in the long run.

To ensure the maintenance staff is adequately utilized during the renovation, start by preparing detailed job descriptions for each team member. Every property has unique maintenance needs, and careful consideration should be given to ongoing maintenance requirements. Providing high-quality service to existing residents can help retain tenants and maximize income when occupancy declines. Reviewing operating expenses under previous management can also provide insight into staffing requirements.

Maintenance personnel also play a role in critical areas of the reposition process, such as unloading and storing materials, installing appliances, and conducting final inspections before unit turnover. This work can quickly be scheduled with the contractor's turnover schedule. There is an added benefit to having maintenance staff perform final checks on each unit, as it means they are familiar with the work that's been done and can address any issues that arise later.

A general guideline is to have one maintenance worker for every 80 to 100 units, but this number will vary depending on the specific tasks required and the workers' competency. Ideally, the maintenance staff should be able to handle both the property's day-to-day maintenance needs and the additional tasks associated with the reposition without requiring significant overtime. As renovation progresses and occupancy increases, the need for additional maintenance staff should decrease, as many extra tasks performed during the renovation will no longer be necessary.

Your policies and procedures for the property should be established as a result of your due diligence efforts. This process should have an analysis of the policies previously in place at the property and those currently used in the local marketplace. Implementing strict, well-enforced policies and procedures for a property undergoing renovation will have a huge impact, like turning a light on in a dark room. Shifting from an absence of policies, or the non-enforcement of existing ones, to firm and fair rules will shock current residents. However, meaningful change can only begin when specific policies are enforced. Establishing these policies is critical to reshaping the property's image and setting the foundation for proper property management operations.

To minimize the shock to residents, it's best to implement these policies in phases. Collection policies, for example, must be enforced within the first 30 days for timely rent payments. Policies addressing criminal activity are equally important, as local law enforcement should deal with unlawful behavior immediately. Relocation policies for tenants and other resident-related procedures must be clearly explained to anyone who queries the management team. New policies and community rules should be presented to residents within the first week of new management, detailing which rules will be replaced, modified, or newly implemented and how they will be enforced.

All policies should be established only after thoroughly researching and evaluating the current market. You must also consider the property's current position in the market and the projected position once the reposition is complete. Policy changes should never be made without careful thought, especially those that will have a lasting impact. The standard operating policies and procedures should address a list of key management functions and resident activities. This will serve as a general guideline for necessary policies at any residential property.

One of the biggest challenges you are likely to face is collections. The new collection policy, or the stricter enforcement of an existing one, should become effective in the month following the takeover, giving residents time to adjust financially. Those accustomed to paying rent late because there were no penalties will need to adapt to the first-of-the-month due date when informed of the new policy and how it will be enforced. This phase-in period may initially increase delinquencies, but swift enforcement will prevent long-term damage and encourage most residents to comply. In addition, tenant-landlord laws may require specific notice periods to ensure compliance with municipal regulations.

A foundational strategy for addressing criminal activity among residents is collaborating closely with local government and law enforcement. During the due diligence phase, it's critical to reach out to police officials to gather information about any known unlawful behavior at the property. Once new management assumes control, inviting law enforcement to help initiate cleanup efforts can be a pivotal first step. Building strong relationships with local authorities not only enhances the property's safety but also signals to the community that positive changes are underway. By swiftly addressing these issues, management fosters a safer living environment and begins reshaping public perception of the property.

In contrast, tenant retention strategies focus on stability and maintaining cash flow. Offering lease renewals to existing residents at the same rate, or with only minor increases, can encourage reliable tenants to stay, especially if reposition projects are expected to extend beyond a year. Retaining tenants who consistently pay on time is invaluable. However, some long-term residents may feel uneasy with the changes brought by new management, and as policies shift to align with the updated vision, some departures may be inevitable.

Still, transitioning to a new resident profile as quickly as possible accelerates improvements in the property's market reputation.

Additionally, you'll need to establish a policy for transferring existing residents into newly renovated units. Although this shouldn't pose significant challenges, the policy must be clear and firm. When renovated units become available, some residents may not be able to afford the increased rent, although some will take advantage of the opportunity. Offering residents a nominal incentive to relocate within the building is good practice. Still, rental discounts should be rarely provided as an incentive to move into a newly renovated unit. Once the unit is occupied, it will never look as good as it does on the day the renovation is complete.

Any discussion of policies would be incomplete without addressing policies regarding staff appearance and dress code requirements. While it may be challenging to enforce a specific dress code without providing uniforms, it is strongly recommended to implement a level of uniformity in the appearance of maintenance workers. Ideally, all maintenance personnel should wear shirts of the same color, provided at the property's expense. Workers should be required to keep these shirts clean, including pin name tags and the property's name. Remember, the property's name may change during renovation, and coordinating colors and uniforms with the new design theme can reinforce the brand's identity. A formal dress code should also be established for the management staff, indicating what is and isn't acceptable business attire, such as prohibiting blue jeans and T-shirts. Clean, professional attire should be mandatory for all staff, regardless of their role on-site.

Employees and staff represent the property to residents and the community. Their appearance is a critical part of the property's professional image. While it is preferable for employees to be salaried to avoid overtime costs, employment laws clearly state that only employees with management responsibilities and those who meet certain criteria can be exempt from overtime pay. Most employees working at the property will be paid an hourly wage and entitled to time-and-a-half for any work over 40 hours per week.

Personnel policies should be explained to all employees upon hiring, and for any staff retained from previous management, these policies should be communicated during the management takeover. These policies should cover areas such as the workday and workweek (including hours worked and break times), pay periods, overtime versus compensatory time, and any benefits. If medical or other insurance benefits are available, employees should be informed whether the employer fully pays them or if contributions are required. It's also advisable to institute a probationary period for all new employees, during which benefits do not accrue. Confirming your policies comply with Equal Employment Opportunity laws will help safeguard against discrimination claims.

These policies are not unique to distressed or value-add properties, but they are necessary for all stabilized properties. In my experience, some employee turnover is expected before you can establish a strong team. Having clear written policies helps facilitate administration and ensures uniform application across the board. All personnel policies should be documented in writing, and each employee should receive a copy. Employees should be required to sign an acknowledgment confirming receipt of this information. When everyone understands the policies, there will be fewer questions and less opportunity for conflict, particularly regarding disciplinary actions or terminations. Clear policies and consistent practices lead to higher morale among staff and contribute to more organized and professional operation.

Most reposition efforts do not require a complete gut job or force existing residents to move out. Much like surgery is a shock to the human body, reposition is a shock to both the property and its residents. There are three property management activities to focus on during a reposition. The first is maintaining continuity of services to existing residents to maximize rental income. The second is evicting residents who do not pay rent or cause problems for management and other tenants. The third is managing the group of residents who occupy units slated for renovation, which will require convincing them to stay and then coordinating their relocation to newly complete apartments. The relocation process will be discussed in more detail elsewhere in this chapter.

The management team must sharpen their people skills during the property's transformation. After establishing management policies and procedures, they must be firm in enforcing the rules, including evicting residents who do not comply. At the same time, management must remain sensitive to the needs of the residents they want to retain. Reposition can be disruptive, and the residents who choose to stay should receive additional services to compensate for the lack of prior attention. Communication is critical here. Residents should be informed of the renovation plans from the outset and updated regularly on the progress and how they will benefit from the changes. Gaining their cooperation early on is essential, and expressing appreciation for their patience throughout the process is crucial.

The best way to manage the inevitable issues during a reposition is to create clear rules and regulations for the residents. These should be simple but enforceable guidelines based on your management policies. While not every rule needs to be enforced immediately, having them in writing is vital, as well as giving all residents a copy. Before creating new rules, understand the existing ones (even if they were not enforced before you took over). Inform residents of the change in management and let them know that any rules already in place will now be implemented.

For example, if residents have been paying rent late because late fees weren't enforced, it would be wise to send a letter reiterating what is stated in the lease. Rent is due on the first of the month and considered delinquent after the fifth, with a late charge applied after that. If this policy hasn't been enforced in a while, it's best to inform residents that it will be strictly followed starting next month. This gives them 20 to 25 days to adjust. Many residents will comply simply because they are reminded of the rule, but some may not. When evictions proceed swiftly and orderly, rent collections will improve.

One eviction can send a potent message to the remaining residents. The key is to ensure the staff understands how to handle the process. Dealing with residents while a property is in transition is challenging at best. How you present and enforce the rules and regulations will determine the type of response you get from your residents. Tough but fair, stern but compassionate, this balance will require fully applying your people skills.

In an earlier chapter, I recommended against using on-site staff to perform construction, but the importance of involving the management team in the reposition process cannot be overstated. There is no better way to build and maintain a strong connection between the construction and property management teams than by having site management routinely assist with the inspection process. Members of the management team, particularly leasing agents, play a major role in re-renting the units and are in direct contact with prospective residents. They hear firsthand feedback on the renovations, yet leasing agents are often left out. This is a mistake, as direct contact with prospects provides valuable insight that can improve the repositions outcome. Management staff also need to stay updated on the progress and quality of the work to relay information to prospects and residents accurately.

Repositioning an apartment property is a team effort; every member should be involved. Managing construction requires continuous inspection both during and after the work is completed. These inspections are frequently conducted to satisfy lender requirements for construction draws but verifying that all work complies with contracts and is completed correctly is paramount. Daily inspections by the site manager and construction management team are also required, not because of any distrust in the contractor but because the management team needs to stay informed about the property's daily progress. This hands-on approach shows interest in the contractor's performance and the overall progress. It also allows the management team to spot potential issues early, which could affect the construction timeline. While contractors occasionally offer solutions to save money or improve the project, the property manager or owner is ultimately responsible for identifying and addressing potential problems.

Inspections can become laborious and repetitive, and it's easy to become complacent over time. To avoid this, use checklists so that all aspects of the inspection are covered thoroughly. Property management is a highly detail-oriented and repetitive business, so checklists and forms are valuable tools to help management personnel focus on their tasks. Although some may argue that too many forms can lead to excessive paperwork, only the necessary forms and checklists should be used during repositioning. While you can't manage from behind a desk, these checklists serve as a guide to make sure nothing is missed during inspections.

Ensuring the management team is adequately trained is the most critical factor in using checklists. They must know how to conduct inspections, what to look for, and how to verify the work's quality. For example, when testing new electrical outlets, an extra two or three minutes spent using a tester can prevent the need for a contractor to return later or create a service request once a new resident moves in. Having maintenance staff address such issues upfront saves on operating costs and prevents inconveniences for new tenants, who you'll want to impress to secure referrals. When routine inspections are performed carefully, inspections for lenders will go smoothly.

You should also establish a clear timeline and defined

chain of command as it will help you complete the renovation project. The construction manager should have direct authority over contractors since they are responsible for paying them, but the site manager will also interact with contractors regularly. At the start of the project, clarify how much authority the site manager will have over the contractors, as the site manager is on the property daily and will often be the primary point of contact. Sometimes, contractors need access to on-site supplies, such as kitchen cabinets. The site manager typically coordinates these supplies. However, the construction manager should be the one authorized to approve project completion.

There should be a clear delineation of who will communicate with the lender, the construction manager will work directly with the sponsor for lender inspections. There should be frequent communication advising the lender of what has happened with the property, good and bad. Anything that requires an alteration to the loan document should be communicated in a face-to-face meeting between the lender and sponsor. Remember, the lender/sponsor relation should be viewed as a long-term proposition.

The critical path method of construction scheduling is based on a series of specific tasks that must be performed in a particular order, with a clear understanding of the time required to complete each. Managing the construction process involves monitoring this critical path, focusing on three categories of potential issues. The first is unforeseen structural or physical problems that may arise as the renovation progresses. These issues must be addressed immediately to avoid delays and keep the project moving as efficiently as possible. This is where the importance of a contingency fund comes into play.

When analyzing a new market, one of the most challenging aspects is the evolving neighborhood and how the market perceives the subject property. As the reposition progresses, the property's marketability may become more substantial than initially anticipated. If this happens, you may need to adjust the construction timetable to accelerate the process. Some items you didn't initially consider can prove critical to improving rental rates and market positioning, while others, like washers and dryers, may not be as necessary. These decisions require careful budget analysis to see if funds are available for such additions or if certain items should be excluded from the reposition.

Unforeseen challenges, such as natural disasters, like fires, tornadoes, or earthquakes, can also disrupt the timeline. Other disruptions, such as material shortages (like the inability to maintain a supply of cabinets) or global events like the COVID pandemic, could create work stoppages that delay the project. If contractors stop working, they may take on other jobs, making them unavailable to resume your project. The goal of the reposition process is to change the image of the property and its perception among residents and the market. The objective of the critical path or construction timeline is to complete the last unit just as the new resident moves in, an ideal scenario. While this is unlikely to happen, ideally, it remains the goal to strive for, as aligning the construction timeline with the property's market perception will ultimately determine the project's success.

The reposition process is inherently unpredictable, and many adjustments to the critical path are likely to be needed as unforeseen circumstances arise. However, keeping a flexible approach and making necessary course corrections will help you stay on track and achieve the desired outcomes for both the property and the market.

In essence, repositioning is a marketing process. By physically transforming a property and adopting new policies and procedures, you create a specific style and environment based on the resident profile you established from your original market analysis. The final manifestation of everything you've accomplished lies in the leasing and renovation of the apartment units. At the outset, your decisions regarding the scope of the reposition, potential name change, the hiring or retention of personnel, and the overall image you want to project will set the tone for the entire process. The new owner faces two opposing goals: achieving the highest possible stabilized occupancy in the shortest time and minimizing cash flow losses. Marketing too early can undermine both objectives.

Reposition will require you to manage a property where renting will continue throughout the renovation. The focus will be on removing non-payers, slow-payers, and lawbreakers while encouraging paying residents to stay. Marketing will continue, but the character of the property and then the resident profile will change gradually. Leasing and renovations will both progress slowly. Exterior and common area improvements should be prioritized, but a full reposition may take three to four years. During this period, the property must wait for the neighborhood's perception to change.

Throughout the reposition process, the outward appearance of a bleak and worn-down property begins to improve, it is natural for those directly involved to feel optimistic. However, expecting the market's perception to change overnight is unrealistic. Prospective residents may still view the property negatively and may be reluctant to make it their home. Additionally, even as physical changes are being made, they may not be immediately favorable. If the initial renovation effort focuses on vacant units, the exterior or surrounding grounds may not immediately show noticeable improvement.

It's also important to remember that prospective residents typically start looking for apartments when their current leases are close to expiring, making an imminent move likely. Most people have difficulty visualizing a property's appearance until the renovation is complete. If only a few units are ready, while the rest of the property remains unimproved, you may lose your opportunity for a positive first impression. Promising future renovations will not convince perspective residents to commit to a lease. This is even more of a challenge for properties undergoing extensive renovation.

Wherever possible, begin the reposition process with fanfare by addressing obvious areas first. Start with exterior cleaning, refinishing, new landscaping, and repairs to the driveway or parking lots. These immediate improvements will signal positive change and help generate enthusiasm. To achieve the highest possible stabilized occupancy in the shortest time, the rent charged must align with your goal. However, premature marketing can be problematic as it increases operating costs, such as additional payroll for leasing staff, without necessarily achieving the proforma rent.

Conversely, delaying marketing for too long can negatively affect staff morale. Leasing staff may become discouraged as their initial excitement about the reposition fades. They may begin to doubt whether the property will be ready for occupancy or if the desired outcome will be achieved. The timing of the rental process must be carefully managed to maintain momentum and ensure success.

The goal of the reposition process should be to complete as much of the common area as possible. Finishing this work signals the market that substantial physical changes are occurring, projecting a new image to the outside world. By this point, most of the visible work will have been completed in areas easily seen by outsiders, and the remaining residents will be qualified rent-paying tenants.

You can also invite community organizations, like the Chamber of Commerce, local real estate professionals, and business owners to tour the property and see the improvements firsthand. It is also the right time to start marketing to the residents who have stayed in their current apartments by mutual agreement. Trying to sell them on the changes before this point is premature, as they need to see the renovation work for themselves before they can appreciate the full impact.

Once they have seen the improvements, those who can

afford the new rents will likely want to stay. To encourage this, you may offer them a small incentive to relocate to a newly renovated unit, although simply moving into a refreshed home should be incentive enough. While some may argue that marketing strategies alone can drive success, the most effective marketing tool is a property that presents well, clearly showing that money has been invested in transforming it.

At this point, it's time to bring in leasing personnel. Initially, you may only need leasing agents working alongside the manager and their assistant. Start an advertising campaign as well but keep it simple. A new property brochure and signage should suffice. Don't underestimate the power of attractive, well-placed digital signage, it's valuable to the property's appeal. Although, avoid relying on promotional gimmicks, giveaways, or rent incentives, as these seldom produce lasting results.

Remember, you're not just selling an apartment but a way of life. The people you're targeting want more than four walls and a roof. They are looking for a place they can proudly call home. In the early stages of marketing, advertising on social media platforms is a great way to reach a broad audience. Avoid using free rent as an enticement and instead highlight unique features of the property, such as window coverings, dishwashers, garbage disposals, dog parks, or built-in shelving. These features will distinguish your property. Include the basics in your advertising, such as unit sizes, square footage, number of bedrooms, bathrooms, and dining areas take the time to describe the units as "newly renovated." It will highlight features, like updated kitchen appliances and new windows. A model unit can also be staged and photographed to showcase how the interiors will look once completed.

A component of your marketing strategy is the person responsible for it. While staff may become enthusiastic about the property because of the changes and your commitment to follow through on the repositioning, they will expect to be compensated for their efforts. Leasing commissions are an excellent way to motivate the staff and maintain their excitement about the project. Two types of incentives can be used, those for individual performance and those for team performance. The type you choose depends on the leasing team's size and the property's specific needs.

Tracking individual commissions can be tricky since a prospect may visit the property several times, interacting with different agents. A team-based approach to leasing and sharing commissions fosters a sense of camaraderie as everyone works together toward the common goal of renting out units. However, team incentives must be substantial enough to be worth dividing among the team members. Before setting up an incentive program, careful thought should be given to factors such as how much commission will be paid, what percentage of the rent it will represent, and what benchmarks must be met to earn these commissions. The property size will also influence the strategy—what works for 200 units may not be effective for a 400-unit property.

When people are deciding where they're going to live, it involves major life changes, like updating their driver's license or voter registration. Due to this, they tend to pay for the best possible service and physical features they can afford. As an apartment marketer, you must rely on this and you need to offer the best service and apartment for the price. Remember, not every prospective resident will have a negative perception of the property, so there's no reason to tell all prospects that the property has had problems in the past. Why sabotage your efforts? Many people new to the area will look at your apartments as objectively as any other complex. Half the battle in leasing is simply getting prospects to visit your property. If the renovation is done well, what they see should be impressive.

Nevertheless, nothing is more disheartening than when a new prospect enthusiastically puts down a deposit only to call a few hours later to say, "I've changed my mind," after hearing negative things about the property. This is likely to happen repeatedly during the early phases of marketing, but leasing staff should be prepared for it and not get discouraged.

There's one clear advantage a fully repositioned apartment property will have over its competition: it's the newest property on the market. The groundwork you've laid in the community, including your ongoing relationships with local government and other stakeholders, will also provide positive feedback in the form of favorable comments to prospective residents asking about your property.

A visually appealing property, well-presented models, and friendly, helpful leasing staff will significantly impact your leasing efforts. These elements are noteworthy to making a positive impression and encouraging prospective residents to sign a lease.

Professional certifications can significantly enhance the skills and credibility of property managers, resulting in improved property performance and increased tenant satisfaction. The Institute of Real Estate and the National Apartment Association provide certifications that demonstrate an individual's commitment to industry's best practices and provide owners and sponsors a confidence in their operators.

One such certification is the Certified Apartment Manager (CAM) Certificate, which offers comprehensive training in property management. This certification covers areas such as marketing, leasing, maintenance, and financial management. To earn the CAM certification, candidates must complete the required coursework, gain relevant professional experience, and pass an examination. This certification is valuable because it holds property managers accountable to adhering to industry standards, which can significantly improve the performance of the property they manage.

Another valuable certification is the Certified Apartment Portfolio Supervisor (CAPS) Certificate, designed for advanced property management professionals overseeing multiple properties. The CAPS certification requires candidates to complete advanced coursework and have substantial experience managing portfolios. By earning this certification, property managers gain advanced knowledge in managing multiple properties, which helps improve operational efficiency and boosts portfolio performance.

Effective management is part of maintaining a well-functioning property and high tenant satisfaction. Regular maintenance and inspections are key components of this. A routine maintenance schedule will keep common areas clean, service HVAC systems, and maintain the curb appeal. In addition to routine upkeep, preventive maintenance is important for identifying potential issues before they escalate into costly repairs. Consistent inspections should be conducted to catch these problems early. Equally important is having a system to handle emergency repairs promptly for tenant safety and overall satisfaction.

Strong tenant relations also play a vital role in effective management. Maintaining open lines of communication is needed, and this can be done through newsletters, emails, and periodic meetings. Responding promptly to tenant inquiries and concerns will build trust and improve retention. When it comes to leasing, strategies, like offering lease renewal incentives or conducting tenant satisfaction surveys can help retain tenants. Additionally, organizing community-building events or activities creates a sense of belonging among residents, further boosting tenant retention.

Financial management is another cornerstone of property operations. Establishing an efficient rent collection system, including offering online payment options, helps ensure timely payments. Monitoring rent payments closely and promptly addressing delinquencies will prevent larger financial issues from developing. Managing the property's budget is equally important. Property managers should track income and expenses carefully and provide quarterly financial reports to investors.

Compliance and risk management are very fundamental to maintaining legal and operational standards. It's essential to ensure the property complies with all relevant local, state, and federal regulations, including fair housing laws and safety standards. In addition, a strong risk management strategy should be implemented. This can include obtaining adequate liability insurance, enhancing security measures, and developing emergency preparedness plans to mitigate potential risks to the property and its residents.

Reporting Made Simple

For consistent and effective management, a monthly property management report can be used to track performance and identify areas for improvement. Here's a template for a typical report:

Property Overview

- Summary of the property's condition and any significant events or issues during the month.

Financial Performance

- Income: Rent collected, other income sources.
- Expenses: Operating expenses, maintenance costs, capital expenditures.
- Net Operating Income (NOI).

Occupancy and Leasing

- Current occupancy rate.
- New leases signed, lease renewals, and tenant turnover.

Maintenance and Repairs

- Summary of maintenance tasks completed.
- List of ongoing or planned repairs and renovations.

Tenant Relations

- Summary of tenant communications and events.
- Feedback from tenant satisfaction surveys.

Compliance and Risk Management

- Updates on legal compliance and any regulatory changes.

Building Tenant Trust

Fostering strong relationships is a cornerstone of successful property management. Effective communication starts at the top in building trust and maintaining satisfaction. Keeping tenants regularly informed through monthly newsletters, emails, and community boards about property updates, maintenance schedules, and community events creates transparency. Also, make sure that property management remains accessible and responsive, addressing tenant inquiries and concerns promptly. Hosting open forums or tenant meetings provides a platform to discuss any issues, gather feedback, and directly address concerns, reinforcing a sense of community and partnership.

Handling tenant concerns or reviews efficiently is another aspect of positive tenant relationships. A streamlined system for managing maintenance requests should be in place, with a focus on resolving issues quickly. Likewise, a clear conflict resolution policy can help address disputes between tenants or between tenants and management. Maintaining a formal complaint management process ensures that every tenant's concern is logged, taken seriously, and resolved appropriately, growing a culture of respect and accountability.

Property managers have the potential to implement various strategies to improve tenant retention. Offering lease renewal incentives, such as carpet cleaning, free upgrades, or extended lease terms, can encourage tenants to stay. Conducting regular tenant satisfaction surveys allows management to gather valuable feedback and identify areas for improvement. Community-building efforts, such as organizing holiday parties, barbecues, or fitness classes, can create a stronger sense of belonging among tenants, making them more likely to renew their leases and remain part of the community.

Managing renovations and rent increases requires balancing the interests of ownership, management, and tenants. From the ownership perspective, the main goal is to enhance property value and increase rental income through strategic renovations. However, ownership faces the challenge of balancing renovation costs with expected returns while managing potential tenant turnover during the renovation process.

For property management, the main challenge lies in balancing occupancy needs with renovation requirements, all while minimizing disruption to tenants. Successful strategies include phasing renovations to reduce tenant inconvenience, clearly communicating with tenants throughout the process, and offering temporary accommodations if necessary to maintain tenant satisfaction.

From the tenant's perspective, renovations and rent increases can cause stress, particularly if they lead to significant disruptions or unexpected financial strain. To mitigate these concerns, clear communication about the benefits of the renovations, such as improved living conditions or enhanced amenities, is essential. Phasing the renovations to minimize inconvenience and addressing tenant concerns quickly can help reduce dissatisfaction so that tenants understand and appreciate the improvements being made to their living environment.

The Maintenance Mindset

Maintenance and repairs will preserve the longevity and safety of multifamily property. By implementing proactive regular maintenance schedules, efficient emergency repair protocols, and thorough property inspections, management can guarantee that the property maintains its value while enhancing tenant satisfaction.

A well-structured maintenance schedule is key to preventing major repairs and keeping the property in good condition. Routine maintenance tasks should include daily activities like cleaning common areas, checking lighting, and addressing minor repairs. Weekly tasks may involve inspecting HVAC systems, testing fire alarms, and maintaining landscaping, while monthly tasks such as servicing elevators, checking plumbing systems, and inspecting roofs and exteriors will help prevent larger issues.

Preventive maintenance is pivotal, with seasonal inspections preparing the property for weather changes, such as checking heating systems in the fall and cooling systems in the spring. Regular service of major equipment, like boilers, water heaters, and HVAC systems, can minimize breakdowns. While long-term planning for tasks, like exterior painting or roof replacement aligns with the property's budget for proper upkeep. Maintaining detailed maintenance logs that record all activities, including dates, tasks performed, materials used, and any issues encountered, will help track the property's maintenance history and inform future strategy.

Emergency repair protocols are also considered a main component of property management. Having a clear plan for handling emergencies ensures tenant safety and lowers damage to the property. Tenants should be provided with clear instructions on how to report emergencies, including contact information for maintenance staff and property management. Moreover, management should maintain a list of reliable vendors and contractors for quick response to emergency repair needs. Develop a response plan that outlines how to assess emergencies and take immediate action, such as shutting off water or electricity.

I prefer having maintenance staff responsible for orienting residents on their move-in day by walking them through their new apartment. During this walkthrough, they should point out essential features like shut-off valves and electrical breakers for emergency situations. This practice not only promotes accountability but also helps maintenance technicians refine their customer service skills.

Additionally, I believe that maintenance should begin their workday by walking the property for the first hour to pick up trash and dog waste. Residents often overlook these details, regardless of the amenities provided. Each month, the staff should perform a thorough cleaning of the property, including the removal of cigarette butts, as it's likely that not everything will be collected during the daily hour. During this time, office staff can organize new work orders or resolve emergencies so the maintenance team has a coordinated plan for the day.

The maintenance supervisor should be an active participant in on-site tasks. If their focus is solely on paperwork and ordering parts, the quality of work from the maintenance team will suffer. When leadership is not willing to engage in the same tasks they assign to their staff, it can lead to resentment among team members.

All emergency repairs should be thoroughly documented, including the issue, actions taken, and any follow-up required. This documentation helps identify recurring issues and improve future responses.

Regular property inspections by regional staff are necessary for identifying maintenance needs, confirming safety, and staying compliant with regulations. Exterior inspections should focus on the building's structure, looking for cracks, signs of water damage, and overall integrity, as well as checking landscaping, walkways, parking areas, and drainage systems. Interior inspections should include common areas like lobbies, hallways, and stairwells to maintain cleanliness and identify any maintenance issues. This is not only about maintenance; it is about being proactive.

Mechanical systems, such as HVAC, plumbing, and electrical systems, must also be regularly inspected for efficiency and safety. Individual unit inspections should focus on plumbing fixtures, electrical outlets, appliances, and the overall condition of each unit. When tenants move out, a detailed turnover inspection will help identify any necessary repairs before new tenants move in. You can do semi-annual unit walks to replace filter, smoke detectors, and batteries.

By adhering to these maintenance and repair strategies, property management can ensure that multifamily properties remain safe, attractive, and fully operational while providing a high level of tenant satisfaction.

Controlling the Costs

Effective expense management is indispensable for maximizing the profitability of a multifamily property. This entails analyzing historical expenses, identifying opportunities for cost savings, and implementing strategies to optimize property expenses without sacrificing quality or tenant satisfaction.

To optimize property expenses, first conduct a thorough expense analysis. This begins with a review of historical expenses to understand spending patterns and pinpoint areas of high costs. Benchmarking the property's expenses against industry standards can also help track where costs may be excessive. The major expense categories typically include utilities, maintenance and repairs, property management fees, insurance, and property taxes.

Utilities in the form of electricity, water, gas, and waste management can account for a significant portion of expenses, but energy-efficient solutions can help reduce these costs. Regular maintenance and repairs, if efficiently scheduled and managed through bulk purchasing, can also lead to savings. Property management fees should be reviewed regularly to make sure they are competitive and in line with the services provided. Additionally, shopping for competitive insurance rates and appealing property tax assessments can further reduce financial burdens.

Several cost-saving measures can be implemented to keep expenses under control. Upgrading to LED or energy-efficient lighting, HVAC (high efficiency) systems, and appliances, as well as installing programmable thermostats and low-flow plumbing fixtures, can significantly diminish utility costs. A preventive maintenance schedule should be followed to avoid costly emergency repairs and extend the lifespan of equipment and systems. It's beneficial to negotiate contracts with vendors and service providers to secure better rates and terms, with long-term or multi-property contracts often offering additional savings. Integrating technology, such as property management software, can streamline operations, reduce administrative costs, and improve overall efficiency.

Hopefully, you have done the bulk of your analysis over your DD period, but more will be revealed as time passes.

The next step is to identify cost drivers. High costs may stem from inefficient systems, security, overstaffing, or frequent repairs caused by poor maintenance. Once they have been determined, an action plan should be developed to address these issues. Solutions may include upgrading equipment, renegotiating contracts, or implementing new policies and procedures to bring expenses under control.

By managing these expenses effectively, property managers can maintain profitability while continuing to deliver high-quality service to tenants.

Math is immutable (except in California). Effective management property is the cornerstone of an operating property. When a property has bad expense management, corporations often raise rents to offset. Some of this is justifying uncontrollable costs, like insurance, utilities, and taxes combined with ineffective expense management of a multifamily asset can destroy the property value.

Innovating for Efficiency

Leveraging technology and implementing innovative solutions is easier today than ever. These advancements can streamline operations, enhance tenant satisfaction, and improve overall property performance. By integrating technology and innovation into multifamily property management, property managers can stay ahead of the curve and optimize their operations.

Property management software plays a large role in streamlining administrative tasks. Software platforms, such as *Yardi*, *AppFolio*, and *Real Page* offer features that include rent collection, maintenance tracking, financial reporting, and tenant communication. The benefits of using these tools are clear: they reduce manual errors, provide real-time data for informed decision-making, and enhance overall efficiency. Additionally, tenant portals offer online access for tenants to pay rent, submit maintenance requests, and communicate with management, which boosts tenant satisfaction by providing convenience and accessibility.

The use of mobile devices enables you to manage tasks on the go, from inspecting properties to responding to tenant inquiries. It also offers a place for data to be retained for the long term. Mobile access improves response times and operational efficiency, making it easier to stay on top of day-to-day responsibilities. Smart home technology is also becoming increasingly popular with devices, like smart thermostats, lighting, and security systems enhancing energy efficiency and providing added convenience for tenants. These devices optimize energy usage, helping to reduce utility costs.

Automating routine tasks, such as lease renewals and maintenance reminders, further reduces the property management workload. Automated systems enhance efficiency by ensuring essential tasks are not overlooked by minimizing manual errors, which helps property managers stay organized.

In terms of tenant services and property operations, modern amenities are a significant draw for prospective tenants. Offering amenities, such as smart gyms, community Wi-Fi, and app-controlled access systems, attracts tech-savvy renters. On the contrary, services like package lockers, fitness centers, and co-working spaces add value to the property and improve tenant satisfaction. Virtual tours and online leasing also streamline the tenant experience. Virtual tours allow prospective tenants to view properties from anywhere, increasing accessibility, and online leasing reduces paperwork and accelerates the move-in process through digital lease signing.

In addition to these foundational tools and concepts, emerging technologies offer advanced solutions for predictive maintenance, enhancing property upkeep with data-driven insights. Predictive maintenance software uses historical data to forecast equipment failures before they happen, allowing property managers to proactively schedule repairs and replacements. For example, HVAC systems with predictive monitoring can alert managers of declining efficiency or parts nearing failure, reducing downtime and preventing costly emergency repairs. This approach not only extends the lifespan of key assets but also minimizes disruptions for tenants by reducing unexpected maintenance visits.

Moreover, AI-driven chatbots and virtual assistants are transforming tenant communication. These tools can handle routine inquiries 24/7, such as answering questions about lease terms, maintenance schedules, or community amenities. For property managers, AI chatbots alleviate the burden on customer service teams and help maintain quick response times, especially during peak times or after hours. Tenants appreciate the convenience of immediate answers and the ability to handle requests at any time. Implementing AI in communication systems supports tenant satisfaction and provides an additional layer of accessibility to property services.

In-unit technology, such as smart appliances, is another innovative feature gaining popularity. Installing energy-efficient appliances like smart refrigerators, washing machines, and dishwashers appeals to environmentally conscious tenants and offers additional control over utility costs. For example, tenants can remotely monitor appliance usage and receive alerts for energy-saving tips or reminders to schedule maintenance. As more tenants look for eco-friendly living options, properties equipped with smart appliances are increasingly attractive, contributing to a greener footprint and fostering long-term tenant retention.

Augmented reality (AR) is also emerging as a tool for property managers and leasing teams. AR can assist maintenance teams in diagnosing equipment issues by overlaying troubleshooting guides directly onto real-world views through smart glasses or mobile devices. Leasing agents can use AR to offer interactive, guided tours, where prospective tenants can visualize furniture placements or see customized finishes without physically visiting the property. These applications not only improve operational efficiency but also create memorable, tech-forward experiences that leave a lasting impression on tenants and prospects alike.

Security innovations, such as AI-powered surveillance systems, are enhancing property safety. These systems can automatically detect unusual activity and alert management or security teams in real time, reducing response times and enhancing tenant safety. Smart cameras, facial recognition for secure access, and AI-driven analytics enable properties to monitor entry points more effectively and respond to security incidents proactively. Such innovations reassure tenants and contribute to a safe, secure living environment, which is a significant factor in tenant satisfaction and retention.

Finally, blockchain technology is finding its way into multifamily property management through secure, transparent transactions. Blockchain can streamline lease agreements, property sales, and rent payments with immutable records, enhancing trust between tenants and management. Digital contracts simplify the leasing process, reduce paperwork, and enable automated renewals, making transactions quicker and more efficient. Blockchain's transparency and security appeal to tenants who prioritize digital privacy and security, and its potential for cost savings benefits property management.

By embracing these innovative technologies, property managers are not only optimizing their daily operations but also setting a forward-thinking standard for tenant experience. These advances make sure properties stay competitive in a rapidly evolving market, aligning with tenant expectations for convenience, sustainability, and digital security. As technology continues to progress, its integration into property management will further redefine the standards for efficient, responsive, and tenant-centered operations.

Your Operational Toolkit

Checklist: Pre-Takeover Planning and Coordination

To ensure a smooth transition, use the following checklist:

Communication With Stakeholders

- Send welcome letters to tenants.
- Hold a town hall meeting with tenants.
- Inform and train existing staff.
- Notify and review vendor contracts.

Operational Setup

- Implement property management software.
- Set up new bank accounts and financial systems.
- Transfer utility accounts and update service contracts.

Staffing and Training

- Evaluate staffing levels and hire additional staff if needed.
- Conduct training programs for new and existing staff.

Maintenance and Repairs

- Conduct initial inspections to identify immediate needs.

- Develop a proactive maintenance schedule.
- Coordinate with vendors to confirm readiness.

Checklist: Tenant Communication and Engagement

To ensure effective tenant communication and engagement, use the following checklist:

Communication

- Regularly update tenants about property improvements and maintenance schedules.
- Maintain open lines of communication through emails, newsletters, and meetings.
- Respond promptly to tenant inquiries and concerns.

Handling Concerns

- Implement an efficient system for handling maintenance requests.
- Develop a clear policy for conflict resolution.
- Maintain a formal process for logging and addressing complaints.

Retention Strategies

- Offer incentives for lease renewal (carpet cleaning).
- Conduct regular tenant satisfaction surveys.
- Organize community events to foster a sense of community.

Checklist for Property Inspections

To ensure thorough and effective inspections, use the following checklist:

Exterior Inspections

- Inspect building structure for cracks and water damage.
- Check landscaping, walkways, and parking areas.
- Assess drainage systems for proper function.

Interior Inspections

- Inspect common areas for cleanliness and maintenance needs.
- Check mechanical systems (HVAC, plumbing, electrical) for proper function.

Unit Inspections

- Inspect plumbing fixtures, electrical outlets, and appliances.
- Check overall unit condition and cleanliness.
- Perform detailed inspections during tenant turnovers.

Template: Annual Maintenance Schedule

An annual maintenance schedule helps organize and plan maintenance tasks throughout the year. This will depend upon the geographic location. Here's a template for a typical annual maintenance schedule:

January:

- Inspect and service heating systems.
- Check for ice buildup on roofs and gutters.

February:

- Inspect plumbing for leaks and insulate pipes.
- Check and clean exhaust fans and vents.

March:

- Inspect roofing and repair any winter damage.
- Prepare landscaping for spring planting.

April:

- Service air conditioning systems.
- Inspect windows and doors for proper sealing.

May:

- Inspect and clean gutters and downspouts.
- Power wash exterior surfaces.

June:

- Inspect and maintain landscaping and irrigation systems.
- Check for pests and schedule pest control if needed.

July:

- Inspect and service HVAC systems.
- Check fire safety equipment.

August:

- Inspect roofing and prepare for fall weather.
- Check exterior lighting and replace bulbs as needed.

September:

- Inspect and seal driveways and parking areas.
- Service heating systems for winter.

October:

- Inspect insulation and weather stripping.
- Clean and inspect chimneys and fireplaces as well as dryer vent cleanouts.

November:

- Inspect and maintain indoor plumbing.
- Check for drafts and seal windows and doors.

December:

- Inspect and maintain emergency generators.
- Check holiday decorations for safety.

Template: Monthly Expense Report

A monthly expense report helps in tracking and managing property expenses effectively. Here's a template for a typical report:

Property Overview
Summary of the property's condition and any significant events or issues during the month.

Income
Rent collected and other income sources.

Expenses
Detailed breakdown of expenses by category (utilities, maintenance, management fees, insurance, property taxes) and comparison to the budgeted amounts.

Net Operating Income (NOI)
It refers to total income minus total expenses.

Variance Analysis
Explanation of any significant variances between actual expenses and budgeted amounts.

Action Plan
Steps to address any overspending and implement cost-saving measures.

Checklist: Technology Integration Plan

To ensure a successful integration of technology and innovation, you can use the following checklist:

Assessment

- Identify current technology gaps and areas for improvement.
- Evaluate the needs and preferences of tenants.

As we close the chapter on operations, it becomes clear that effective management leads to the long-term success of any real estate investment. The smooth operation of a property can mean the difference between consistent cash flow and a property that struggles to meet its financial obligations. From maintaining the physical structure to managing tenant relationships, every aspect of operations must be handled with discipline and foresight. Whether you decide to manage the property yourself or hire a management company, understanding the key operational elements is vital.

Operations encompass a wide range of responsibilities, including managing maintenance schedules, controlling costs, maintaining regulatory compliance, and addressing tenant needs promptly. A well-managed property not only retains its value but also attracts and retains high-quality tenants. This reduces vacancy rates and turnover, ultimately boosting profitability. As we have explored, being proactive in property maintenance and communication with tenants fosters a positive environment, which is essential for operational success.

With operations functioning smoothly, it's also important to maintain a long-term view of your investment. While operations focus on the present, eventually, every investment property reaches the stage where you'll need to consider your exit strategy. Whether it's due to market conditions, a need to free up capital, or simply the right time to sell, the disposition phase is the next logical step in the lifecycle of your investment.

The disposition phase marks the final chapter in your investment cycle, where you decide to sell or refinance the property. Disposition is not just about finding a buyer; it involves careful planning to maximize your returns and ensure that the sale aligns with your long-term financial goals. Timing, market conditions, and asset performance all play critical roles in this decision.

In the upcoming chapter, we'll explore the main considerations involved in successfully navigating the disposition phase. From preparing the property for sale to selecting the right selling strategy, we'll guide you through the steps necessary to exit your investment with confidence and profitability.

CHAPTER 5

Mastering the Exit

Every investment has an endpoint, and in the multifamily asset management space, this is known as the disposition phase. Whether you're selling a property to realize gains or refinance as a part of a broader portfolio strategy, disposition is a critical stage that demands as much attention as the acquisition and operational phases. It's not just about putting a "for sale" sign on the property; it's about timing the sale to align with market conditions, maximizing the asset's value, and ensuring a smooth transition for both the buyer and your team.

In this chapter, we'll explore the strategies behind a successful disposition, from preparing a property for sale and conducting a detailed financial analysis to selecting the right brokerage team and navigating the complexities of negotiations. We'll also examine case studies that highlight how well-executed disposition plans can significantly boost returns. By the end of this chapter, you'll understand how to structure your exit strategy to maximize value, protect your investment, and secure long-term financial growth.

When managing multifamily properties, owners and investors often face a pivotal decision: whether to sell (disposition) or refinance the property. Both options come with distinct advantages and disadvantages, and the choice depends on the investor's financial goals, market conditions, and long-term strategy. Here's a comparison of disposition and refinance to help clarify their differences and potential impacts on property management:

Disposition, or selling the property, is a strategy used when investors believe it is the optimal time to exit and realize their profits. The goal of disposition is to maximize returns by selling the property at the most advantageous time based on market conditions. When market conditions are favorable, disposition allows investors to lock in profits, especially in a hot real estate market or when the property has appreciated significantly. Market timing is key, and a thorough analysis of economic trends, interest rates, and property demand is necessary for the highest possible sale price.

Another major benefit of disposition is the liquidity it provides. Once the sale is complete, investors can access the capital, reinvest it in other opportunities, or distribute returns to stakeholders. Disposition is usually part of a long-term exit strategy, where investors plan to sell after achieving their target financial objectives. It may also be the right choice for those looking to reduce risk exposure or shift capital into other ventures.

However, one drawback of selling a property is the potential tax implications. Disposition may trigger significant taxes. To mitigate this, investors can potentially use a 1031 Exchange, where the proceeds are reinvested in a new property, deferring tax liabilities.

Refinance refers to obtaining new permanent financing for an asset to take advantage of better loan terms, lower interest rates, or to extract equity without selling the property. This option allows investors to retain ownership while, often, improving their financial position.

Lower interest rates can reduce monthly mortgage payments, improve cash flow, and potentially result in better loan terms, such as extending the loan duration or restructuring debt. Equity extraction from refinancing allows property owners to tap into the increased value of the property due to the repositioning process by accessing the value that has been created.

Unlike disposition, refinancing does not typically trigger capital gains taxes, making it a more tax-efficient option for investors who want to access liquidity without selling the property. Market timing is also important in identifying the optimal selling window. By analyzing market conditions and economic trends, investors and property managers can assess when to sell the property to maximize profitability

Strategic planning is at the core of an effective disposition process. Developing a comprehensive exit strategy ensures the sale aligns with financial goals and market conditions. This strategy typically includes property valuation, marketing efforts, and negotiation techniques so that every aspect of the sale is optimized for success.

Disposition primary components begin with exit strategy development, which focuses on planning the sale from the outset. By aligning the sale with financial objectives and the state of the market, sponsors can confirm they are prepared to sell at the most favorable time. Market timing involves assessing both current and projected market conditions to determine when the sale should take place.

Another critical element is marketing the property. Creating a comprehensive marketing plan is essential for attracting potential buyers and maximizing property exposure, so that the property stands out in a competitive market. Following this, negotiating the sale requires effective strategies to secure favorable terms and maximize the sale price, contributing directly to the success of the transaction.

A successful disposition strategy also involves careful financial planning and forecasting. Assessing potential returns from the sale helps investors and managers understand the property's true value in the current market. Additionally, calculating expenses related to the sale, including brokerage fees, legal costs, and potential taxes, provides a clear picture of the net gain. This thorough financial analysis supports informed decision-making and ensures that the final disposition aligns with long-term financial objectives.

Finally, closing the transaction involves managing the process to make sure all legal and financial obligations are met. This includes overseeing the distribution of funds for a smooth transition between the seller and buyer. By focusing on these components, property managers can execute successful dispositions that meet financial goals and optimize returns.

The choice between disposition and refinance depends on the investor's long-term goals, the financial health of the property, and current market conditions. Disposition is the better option for investors looking to exit a property, maximize profits, and reinvest or realize liquidity. Refinance, on the other hand, allows for continued ownership and can improve cash flow, reduce loan costs, and provide access to equity without selling. Each strategy has its own merits and tax implications, and the right choice will depend on the investor's overall portfolio strategy and market outlook.

Timing the Peak

Timing the market correctly comes in handy for maximizing returns when selling a multifamily property. This process entails assessing current market conditions, evaluating economic indicators, and making informed decisions about the best time to list the property. Understanding these factors allows sponsors to capitalize on favorable market dynamics and achieve the highest possible sale price.

- Specific Indicators to look for on both a Macro and Micro perspective:
    - Inflation
    - Interest rates
    - Equity availability
    - Job growth
    - Population growth
    - New construction

One of the first steps in assessing market conditions is to monitor current property values in the local area to determine whether they are trending upward or downward. Property values are an indicator of the market's health and can signal the optimal time to sell. Additionally, evaluating rental rates and occupancy levels provides insight into the demand for rental properties, which influences buyer interest. Analyzing recent sales activity is also a big factor in gauging competition and the level of buyer engagement in the market.

Lessons From Market Cycles: Peaks and Valleys

The real estate market is anything but linear. From the economic turmoil of 2007 to 2009 to the unprecedented frothing market of 2021, history teaches us the value of preparation and adaptability. Between 2007 and 2009, the market plummeted from a booming high, fueled by condo conversions and record-low interest rates, to a historic low that inspired films like The Big Short. My family experienced this firsthand during a conversion project in Reno, Nevada. As the market collapsed, we were left holding a fractured property, straddling apartments and condos. It was a textbook example of market vulnerability, and it underscored the importance of having a clear plan and sufficient reserves.

By contrast, 2021 was a period of relentless optimism, with interest rates at historic lows and equity pouring into real estate. CAP rates compressed to unprecedented levels, and deals closed at razor-thin margins. In Phoenix, we completed a transaction at a 1.8% cap rate on actuals, a testament to the speculative environment. Hindsight is the best judge but recognizing market froth and knowing when to exit is an invaluable skill. Selling in a booming market typically means capitalizing on perceived value rather than actual performance, a lesson we leveraged successfully.

The Science of Market Timing

Market timing is more than guesswork; it requires staying in tune with local trends and national shifts. Certain factors, like military base closures or oversupply in small markets, can create unique challenges. Conversely, strong job growth or infrastructure investments can ignite demand in unexpected areas. Being first through the wall during a downturn is often bloody, but calculated risks backed by solid data analysis can yield outsized rewards. The key is preparation: understanding reserve requirements, conducting thorough due diligence, and building a flexible strategy.

In 2022, the market entered a new phase. Rising interest rates, growing inflation, and an overabundance of capital collided with supply shortages exacerbated by COVID. Delinquency and low cash flow became common challenges in a market bloated by excessive valuations. These shifts reinforced the importance of discipline and the dangers of ego-driven decision-making in real estate investment.

Emotion-Free Decision-Making

One of the aspects I appreciate most about multifamily transactions is their reliance on numbers rather than emotion. Unlike single-family homebuyers, investors in multifamily real estate are driven by financial performance. This lack of emotional attachment allows for clear-eyed decisions and the ability to walk away when necessary. Financial data and due diligence form the foundation of every decision to keep transactions grounded in reality.

However, market timing isn't solely about avoiding mistakes, it's about seizing opportunities. Selling in a booming market, for instance, allows investors to command a premium for perceived value. A buyer may pay for renovations completed on just 10% of units as if 30% had been renovated, a phenomenon that underscores the importance of strategic marketing and timing. Creating a competitive bidding environment can further enhance sale prices, ensuring the property commands top dollar.

Real estate is as much an art as it is a science. Timing the market requires discipline, preparation, and the ability to adapt to changing conditions. Ego has no place in this business; data and discipline are far more reliable guides. Whether navigating the peaks of a frothy market or the valleys of a downturn, having a clear plan and a long-term vision supports success. As my old chess teacher advised, "If you don't have three moves planned, stop and make a plan." In real estate, as in chess, strategy is everything.

Economic indicators are another element of market timing. Changes in interest rates can significantly impact buyers' purchasing power, influencing the overall activity in the real estate market. Higher interest rates typically reduce buyer demand, making it a less favorable time to sell. Employment rates are equally important, as strong job growth and low unemployment tend to drive up demand for housing. Similarly, inflation rates should be monitored closely, as they can affect both operational costs and property values.

The dynamics of supply and demand also play a role in determining the right time to sell. Keeping an eye on new developments and construction projects can increase the supply of rental properties and potentially lower demand for existing ones. Analyzing absorption rates and the speed at which new rental units are being leased provides further insight into how quickly the market is absorbing new inventory and helps assess the balance between supply and demand.

In addition to current market conditions, evaluating future projections is critical to strategic decision-making. Economic forecasts, which offer predictions about potential growth or downturns in both the local and national economy, provide valuable context for determining the best time to sell. Industry reports from sources like CoStar, Yardi Matrix, and the National Apartment Association can also offer insights into upcoming market trends, helping investors anticipate changes in demand or pricing.

Demographic trends should not be overlooked when timing a property sale. Population growth projections, for example, can signal increasing demand for housing, while shifts in demographics, such as an aging population or changing household sizes, can alter housing preferences. These factors can greatly influence the demand for multifamily properties.

Lastly, you need to stay informed about your potential policy changes. Regulatory changes, zoning laws, tax policies, and housing regulations can all affect the real estate market, sometimes creating either favorable or unfavorable conditions for selling. Government initiatives aimed at stimulating housing or economic growth can also present opportunities for investors to capitalize on favorable market conditions.

To maximize returns when selling a multifamily property, understanding buyer sentiment is an important factor in market timing. Investor sentiment often reflects broader economic confidence and can impact the pace and price at which properties sell. For instance, when investors are optimistic about the economy, they may be more willing to pay premium prices for assets. By comparison, during times of economic uncertainty or volatile stock markets, investors may lean toward more conservative offers or delay their acquisitions, impacting the final sale price. Monitoring investor sentiment through industry surveys and market reports can help you gauge the prevailing mood and determine whether the market is favorable.

In addition, keeping an eye on capital markets is essential. Market liquidity can significantly impact the pool of potential buyers and, consequently, property values. When financing is readily available and lenders are actively seeking to fund real estate deals, buyers are more likely to enter the market, which can create favorable selling conditions. Conversely, if lenders tighten their lending criteria due to economic concerns, buyer numbers may decrease, potentially making it more challenging to secure an attractive offer. Understanding the lending environment by consulting with financial institutions or mortgage brokers can provide insight into whether capital is likely to flow into or out of the market.

Seasonal market fluctuations are another consideration for timing your sale. Typically, spring and early summer are considered peak seasons for property sales, as favorable weather and relocation trends encourage higher buyer activity. On the other hand, buyer interest can wane in late fall and winter. While multifamily properties don't strictly follow the same seasonal patterns as single-family homes, adjusting your timing to align with periods of higher demand can help attract more offers. Additionally, adjusting to buyer availability around major holidays or end-of-year budgeting timelines may increase the likelihood of a quicker sale.

Equity appreciation and tax implications should also be factored into timing considerations. For instance, holding onto a property for a slightly longer period may result in significant appreciation in a thriving market. Understanding capital gains tax implications or possible tax incentives for holding a property over a specific duration can also affect your timing. Working with a tax advisor can help clarify the benefits of various timing strategies from a tax perspective, allowing you to time your sale for both maximum profit and tax efficiency.

Finally, preparing a property for sale is an integral part of market timing. Ensuring the property is in an optimal condition and that any deferred maintenance issues are addressed can increase its appeal to prospective buyers. Completing improvements or renovations that align with current market demands can elevate the property's value, making it more competitive. For example, enhancing curb appeal, upgrading units with popular amenities, or modernizing common areas can make a significant difference in the property's perceived value. A property that presents well and meets market standards is more likely to attract strong offers, especially if listed at a strategic time.

In summary, timing the market correctly is a vital component of maximizing returns when selling a multifamily property. By carefully assessing market conditions, evaluating key economic indicators, and considering future projections, investors can make informed decisions about the optimal time to list their property.

The Selling Strategy

Creating a comprehensive marketing plan can help you attract potential buyers and maximize the sale price of a multifamily property. Effective marketing involves showcasing the property's strengths, utilizing various marketing techniques, and targeting the right audience for a successful sale.

The first step in developing a marketing plan is knowing the target audience. It's important to determine the type of investors who would be interested in the property, such as individual investors, real estate investment trusts (REITs), or private equity firms. By analyzing demographic data, sponsors can better understand the characteristics of potential buyers and tailor their marketing strategy accordingly.

Once the target audience is identified, the next step is to highlight the selling points of the property. Emphasizing unique property features, such as modern amenities, recent renovations, energy-efficient systems, and desirable unit layouts that set the property apart from others on the market. Additionally, showcasing the benefits of the property's location, its proximity to employment centers, schools, public transportation, and local attractions can increase its appeal. Offering detailed information on the property's financial performance, including occupancy rates, rental income, and historical financial statements, is also crucial for capturing the interest of serious buyers.

Creating effective marketing materials is another good component. Developing a professional offering memorandum that includes property details, financial performance, market analysis, and investment highlights will serve as a comprehensive resource for potential buyers. Digital marketing tools, such as a property website, virtual tours, high-quality photos, and videos, should be utilized to give buyers an immersive experience of the property. Print materials, including brochures, flyers, and posters, are also useful for distribution at industry events and meetings to further promote the property.

Another major factor to keep in mind is the timeline. Establishing a timeline for the marketing campaign will maintain momentum and attract a steady stream of interest in the property. Outlining milestones, such as launch dates for online listings, email campaign rollouts, and scheduled networking events, helps keep the marketing strategy on track and maximizes exposure to potential buyers.

Striking the Deal

Effective negotiation strategies should not be neglected for maximizing the sale price and achieving favorable terms when selling a multifamily property. Understanding buyer motivations, preparing thoroughly, and employing strategic negotiation techniques can lead to a successful transaction.

Understanding buyer motivation is the foremost step in crafting a strong negotiation approach. Many buyers focus on their investment goals, particularly the return on investment (ROI) and cash flow. Highlighting the property's strong financial performance and future growth potential can make it more appealing to these buyers. Moreover, some buyers are looking for repositioning opportunities, meaning they are interested in properties where they can make improvements to increase value and rental income. Emphasizing renovation or expansion possibilities can be a key selling point. *Leave some meat on the bone for the next guy.*

Market conditions also play a significant role in buyer motivation. Buyers prefer markets with stability, low vacancies, and high demand for rental units. Providing data on the local market's stability and growth prospects can help reassure them. Similarly, showcasing the property's competitive advantage over others on the market, such as unique features or a prime location, can set the property apart.

Financing and risk concerns are often top of mind for buyers. Offering information about the property's eligibility for attractive financing terms can make the deal more appealing. Buyers are also interested in how potential risks are mitigated, whether through strong tenant covenants, property insurance, or robust maintenance programs, as this helps reduce their perceived financial exposure.

Preparation for negotiation is also mandatory for a successful sale. Start by gathering information, including a clear understanding of the property's market value based on comparable sales and income analysis. Detailed financial statements, Rent Rolls, and historical income and expense reports should be prepared to support the asking price. Compile market data that includes trends in rental rates, occupancy levels, and property values to further justify the property's pricing and potential, you are selling a dream.

Before entering negotiations, you need to set objectives. Determine the minimum acceptable price and desired terms, including any contingencies or conditions for the sale. Identifying areas where concessions might be acceptable, such as closing costs or minor repairs, can help facilitate smoother negotiations. Additionally, building rapport with potential buyers is essential. Clear and open communication helps establish a positive relationship, allowing sponsors to understand the buyer's needs and concerns, which can help in building trust. Maintain professionalism throughout the negotiation process so that all interactions remain respectful and constructive.

When employing negotiation strategies, start strong. Present a solid initial offer that reflects the property's value, leaving room for negotiation, and being prepared to justify the asking price with supporting data and analysis. Flexibility is key; showing a willingness to negotiate on terms important to the buyer can lead to a favorable outcome. It's also critical to highlight the property's value by emphasizing unique features, recent improvements, and strong financial performance. Using data and visual aids, such as charts and graphs, can help reinforce these points. Additionally, discussing the property's future potential and how it aligns with potential investment goals can strengthen the appeal.

As with any negotiation, managing objections is a necessary skill. Listening to the prospect's concerns and addressing them directly with information and potential solutions can keep the negotiation moving forward. Be prepared to offer concessions, such as minor repairs or flexible closing dates, to address concerns and facilitate a smoother transaction.

Closing the deal is the final step. Once a mutual agreement is reached, confirm that all terms are clearly documented in a written agreement. Maintaining communication and following through on agreed terms leads to a smooth closing process and a successful sale.

In simple words, effective negotiation strategies are key to maximizing the sale price and achieving favorable terms when selling a multifamily property. By understanding buyer motivations, preparing thoroughly, and employing strategic negotiation techniques, sponsors can secure successful transactions.

The Final Handoff

Closing the transaction is the final step in the sale of a multifamily property. This stage is all about coordinating with different parties, making sure all legal and financial documents are in order, and addressing any last-minute issues that may arise. A well-managed closing process generally means a smooth and successful transaction, and attention to detail during this phase can prevent delays and complications.

Managing the closing process requires coordination with all relevant parties, which is usually done by the title company. Maintaining open communication with both buyers and sellers ensures that all terms and conditions are understood and agreed upon. Working closely with attorneys and legal counsel is also essential for reviewing and finalizing legal documents, such as the purchase agreement, deed, and any necessary disclosures. Coordination with the title company is necessary for a clear title to be transferred to the buyer and for title insurance to be secured.

In terms of financial arrangements, ensure all loan documentation is reviewed and signed. This includes the mortgage agreement, promissory note, and any other financing-related paperwork. Establishing an escrow account is also vital to managing the transfer of funds so that all payments, including the purchase price, closing costs, and prorated expenses, are handled properly and securely.

A final walkthrough of the property should be conducted with the buyer to confirm that it is in the agreed-upon condition and that any required repairs have been completed. Review the final inspection reports to verify that all contingencies have been met and avoid any surprises or disputes at the closing table.

You can see the full file by using the QR code.

Seller's Settlement Statement

Settlement Date: **File No:** [redacted]
Officer: [redacted]

Description	Seller Charge	Seller Credit
Legal Fees [redacted]	39,741.11	
Legal Fees [redacted]	1,034.55	
Payment [redacted]	6,500.00	
Asset Management [redacted]	2,934.64	
Proceeds to [redacted]	10,485,871.14	
Real Estate Broker Charges		
Commission [redacted]	196,721.31	
Totals	24,591,141.67	24,591,141.67

PLEASE NOTE: A modification of money-transfer or disbursement instructions can be a red flag for Online Banking Fraud and could be a trap for the unwary. Should we knowingly receive such a modification, in the interest of prudence, we may consider it suspect and call a known and trusted phone number to verify its authenticity and accuracy. Your awareness and cooperation in taking appropriate steps to prevent fraud is greatly appreciated.

See Attached Signatures

When it comes to signing and transferring ownership, arranging for all parties to sign the necessary documents is the final step. This can be done either in person or electronically, depending on the preferences and location of the parties involved. Ensuring that the deed transfer is properly executed, notarized, and recorded with the local government is key to officially transferring ownership of the property to the buyer.

Throughout the process, be prepared for potential challenges. One of the most common issues is related to the property's title. Verify that there are no liens, encumbrances, or title defects that could affect the transfer of ownership. Title insurance should be obtained to protect against future claims or disputes regarding the property's ownership.

Financing delays can also pose a challenge, so it is important to verify that the buyer's loan is approved in a timely manner. Addressing any financing contingencies promptly will help avoid delays in closing. Similarly, verifying that all repairs and maintenance tasks have been completed to the buyer's satisfaction to avoid last-minute issues. If necessary, escrow holdbacks can be negotiated to cover incomplete repairs, so they are resolved after closing.

Addressing any compliance and legal issues is a vital part

of the closing process. Making sure that the transaction complies with local, state, and federal regulations helps avoid legal complications. Should any disputes arise, they must be resolved promptly with the help of legal counsel, so the transaction proceeds smoothly.

Clear communication and meticulous planning are essential for a successful close in multifamily property transactions. Setting realistic timelines for document review, funds transfer, and the completion of final inspections helps minimize stress and prevent unforeseen delays so that every party involved understands these timelines and their responsibilities is crucial for a smooth transition.

The coordination of utility transfers and property management handover is another detail often addressed during closing. Arranging for the seamless transfer of utility accounts to the new owner, along with introducing the buyer to property management teams, sets a solid foundation for post-transaction operations. In cases where tenant leases are involved, informing tenants of ownership changes and confirming lease documentation is current can aid in a smooth transition for everyone affected.

Finally, the post-closing phase involves achieving all transaction documents, verifying the release of funds from escrow, and confirming that title transfer is formally recorded. These final confirmations close out the transaction and ensure a complete and clean transfer of ownership.

By coordinating with all parties, managing financial arrangements, checking due diligence, preparing necessary documents, and addressing potential challenges, sponsors assist in a smooth and successful closing process.

Sharing the Success

Disbursing funds is the final step in the closing process of a multifamily property transaction. It involves guaranteeing that all financial obligations are met, funds are properly allocated, and all parties receive their due payments. A well-managed disbursement process guarantees a smooth transition of ownership and satisfies all financial agreements made during the sale.

Managing escrow accounts is central to the disbursement process. First, an escrow account is established to hold the funds until all conditions of the sale are met, providing security for both the buyer and the seller. Selecting a reputable escrow agent or title company is essential for an efficiently managed account and that funds are disbursed according to the sales agreement.

Deposits and transfers into the escrow account begin with the buyer making an initial deposit, known as earnest money, to demonstrate their commitment to the transaction. At closing, the buyer then transfers the final purchase funds, which include the purchase price and any closing costs. Before disbursing the funds, the escrow agent reviews all closing documents to verify that the conditions of the sale have been met, and both the buyer and seller must provide approval to proceed.

Disbursing funds involves several steps, starting with the payment of liens and debts. The sale proceeds are used to pay off any outstanding mortgages or loans secured by the property, ensuring the buyer receives a clear title. Additionally, any property liens or encumbrances must be settled to avoid future disputes.

The next step is the settlement of closing costs, which includes covering title fees for title insurance and searches, escrow fees for the services provided by the escrow agent or title company and recording fees for filing the deed and other legal documents with the local government. Once these costs are paid, commission payments are disbursed to real estate agents or brokers, as specified in the sales contract.

The disbursement process also involves handling prorated expenses, such as property taxes and any utilities or other prorated fees. These are adjusted based on the closing date. Generally, both the buyer and seller pay their fair share of these expenses.

Finally, the final distribution of funds occurs. The seller's proceeds are transferred from the escrow account once all obligations and expenses have been paid.

Insights for the Future

Reflecting on the entire investment process of a multifamily property is important for identifying successes, areas for improvement, and best practices. This reflection informs future investments and enhances the overall strategy for property management and disposition.

Successes in the investment process began with effective underwriting. A comprehensive underwriting process incorporated detailed market analysis, financial projections, and risk assessments. The accuracy of the initial financial projections, which closely matched the actual outcomes, further demonstrated the effectiveness of the model.

The investment also benefited from comprehensive due diligence. Detailed inspections were conducted, identifying potential issues early and allowing for proactive management. Additionally, thorough legal and financial due diligence ensured a clear title transfer, compliance with all regulations, and validation of the property's financial health.

A smooth transition and management phase followed. A detailed transition plan facilitated a seamless takeover, guaranteeing tenant satisfaction and operational continuity. The implementation of effective property management practices, including regular maintenance and proactive tenant relations, led to high occupancy rates and strong tenant retention.

Strategic marketing and sales efforts were another highlight. A targeted marketing plan attracted prospects and, eventually, buyers by utilizing professional photography, virtual tours, and online listings. This was supported by successful negotiation strategies, which maximized the sale price and secured favorable terms.

Finally, the investment saw an efficient closing process. Close coordination with all parties assured that all financial obligations were met, and funds were disbursed correctly.

Detailed documentation and clear communication helped minimize delays and resolve any issues promptly.

Risk management also presented opportunities for improvement. Diversifying investments across different markets or property types could help mitigate market-specific risks. Developing more robust contingency plans for unexpected events, such as economic downturns or regulatory changes, would enhance resilience and safeguard the investment.

Looking ahead, several best practices emerged. Thorough due diligence remains critical. A disciplined approach to physical, environmental, legal, and financial aspects creates informed decision-making and risk mitigation. Using checklists and templates helps standardize the due diligence process and ensures all critical areas are covered.

Maintaining effective communication is another best practice. Engaging stakeholders, including tenants, staff, and vendors, with clear and consistent communication builds transparency and trust. Proper documentation of all processes, decisions, and communications aids in tracking progress and resolving disputes.

In addition to the previously identified successes and areas for improvement, the lessons learned from the investment process highlight the importance of building a strong team. Collaboration among experienced professionals, including property staff, real estate agents, financial analysts, and legal advisors, proved invaluable. Each team member brought unique expertise, leading to comprehensive oversight throughout the investment cycle. Regular team meetings fostered open communication, allowing for the swift identification and resolution of issues while also promoting innovative ideas that contributed to the investment's success.

Another critical lesson learned is the value of tenant feedback in shaping property management strategies. Engaging tenants through surveys or informal check-ins provided valuable insights into their needs and preferences. Understanding tenant experiences allowed for tailored improvements in property management, enhancing overall satisfaction. Implementing tenant feedback not only improved retention rates but also encouraged a sense of community within the property, encouraging tenants to recommend the property to others.

In terms of financial management, establishing a robust budgeting process was pivotal. Regular reviews of operating expenses and comparisons against budgeted figures helped identify discrepancies early. This proactive approach allowed for timely adjustments and cost-saving measures, ensuring that the property remained financially viable. Implementing a rigorous financial monitoring system also facilitated timely responses to market changes, allowing for quicker pivots when necessary.

Finally, embracing adaptability emerged as a crucial lesson. The ability to pivot strategies in response to changing market conditions or tenant needs allowed for continued success throughout the investment cycle. For example, during economic fluctuations, the management team adjusted marketing strategies to focus on value-oriented messaging, attracting tenants looking for affordable housing options. Being open to change and responsive to feedback from both tenants and the market will remain essential for future investments.

Reflecting on the multifamily property investment process yields valuable insights that can enhance future strategies. From emphasizing team collaboration and tenant engagement to leveraging technology and sustainability practices, these lessons learned will inform and guide decision-making in subsequent investments. By continually assessing successes and areas for improvement, sponsors can refine their approaches and position themselves for sustained success in a dynamic real estate market.

Remember, successful disposition relies on strategic timing, an understanding of the market, and the proper preparation of your asset for sale. Throughout this phase, working closely with brokers, legal professionals, and accountants means that your sales proceed smoothly and that you remain compliant with financial and tax regulations. As you prepare to transition out of this investment, take stock of what you've learned throughout the entire process, from acquisition, operations, and now through to disposition. These lessons will inform your future investments, equipping you with the knowledge and experience to optimize your real estate portfolio.

Exiting your investment is not just an end but a transformation, an opportunity to build upon the value you've created and leverage that into your next venture. Whether you choose to reinvest or diversify, the disposition phase offers a moment to reflect on the achievements and challenges of this project and how it will influence your next steps in the real estate market.

THE FINAL TAKEAWAY

As we conclude our exploration of multifamily asset management and sponsorship, it becomes clear that the journey through this intricate landscape demands a thorough multifaceted understanding of various interconnected components, from apartment sponsorship to the intricacies of operations and disposition strategies. This comprehensive guide has explained the fundamental concepts and practical applications necessary for success in the multifamily sector, emphasizing the importance of each stage in the reposition process.

The initial chapter laid the groundwork by defining apartment sponsorship, a critical component that facilitates the acquisition and management of multifamily properties. By acting as the bridge between investors and operators, sponsors not only provide the necessary capital but also bring their expertise and credibility to the table. This relationship is important for navigating the complexities of the real estate market so that projects are viable and aligned with investor expectations. Understanding the dynamics of sponsorship is vital for anyone looking to engage in multifamily investment.

Moving into the underwriting phase, we discussed the analytical processes that assess the financial viability of a multifamily investment. Underwriting is not merely about crunching numbers; it encompasses a deep dive into market trends, property performance, and risk assessment. A disciplined underwriting process enables sponsors to make informed decisions, set realistic projections, and establish a sound financial framework for the property. By employing rigorous due diligence, sponsors can uncover potential pitfalls and capitalize on opportunities, thus ensuring that investments yield favorable returns. The insights gained during this phase ultimately form the foundation for the operational strategies that follow.

Due diligence emerged as another step that precedes any acquisition or investment decision. This chapter underscored the importance of a thorough investigation into a property's legal, financial, and physical aspects. It is during this phase that potential risks are identified and mitigated, ensuring that investors are equipped with all the necessary information to make educated choices. By implementing comprehensive due diligence practices, sponsors not only protect their investments but also enhance the long-term value of the properties they manage. The lessons learned here can significantly influence subsequent operations and strategic decisions.

With a solid foundation established, we transitioned to the operational aspects of multifamily asset management. This chapter highlighted the necessity of effective property management, tenant relations, and maintenance strategies. Successful operations are integral to maximizing property value and ensuring tenant satisfaction. Implementing best practices in leasing, resident engagement, and service delivery can lead to higher occupancy rates and increased revenue. The significance of operations cannot be overstated, as it directly impacts the overall performance and reputation of the property in a competitive market.

Finally, we explored the disposition process, where strategic decisions about the sale or refinancing of a property come into play. Understanding the market dynamics at this stage is pivotal for optimizing returns on investment. A well-timed disposition, informed by comprehensive market analysis and operational performance, can yield significant profits for investors. Additionally, this chapter emphasized the notion that foresight and planning are essential to successful multifamily asset management.

Through these chapters, a clear theme emerged: the interconnectedness of each component of multifamily sponsorship. From underwriting to disposition, every aspect of the process is interwoven, and a misstep in one area can reverberate throughout the entire operation. This disciplined understanding equips sponsors with the foresight to anticipate challenges and leverage opportunities, ultimately contributing to the sustained success of multifamily properties.

Looking ahead, it is important to acknowledge the ever-evolving nature of the multifamily real estate market. Emerging trends, such as the integration of technology in property management, shifts in tenant demographics, and changing economic landscapes, present both challenges and opportunities for sponsors. Staying informed of these trends and adapting strategies accordingly will be paramount for long-term success. Embracing change and being proactive in implementing innovative solutions will set successful sponsors apart in this competitive environment.

Know that multifamily sponsorship is a multifaceted discipline that requires a deep understanding of various components, from the initial stages of underwriting to the complexities of operations and eventual disposition. This comprehensive guide aims to equip readers with the knowledge and tools necessary to navigate this intricate landscape successfully. By emphasizing the interconnectedness of each aspect, the importance of rigorous analysis, and the need for strategic foresight, I hope to inspire confidence in aspiring sponsors.

As you embark on your journey in multifamily, remember that the relationships you cultivate and the positive impact you create within the communities you serve are what truly matters. The multifamily sector offers immense potential for growth and fulfillment, and by applying the principles outlined in this guide, you can contribute to the creation of vibrant, thriving living environments for residents while achieving your investment goals.

In this dynamic field, continuous learning and adaptation are key. Engage with industry experts, participate in professional development opportunities, and stay informed about market trends. The insights gained from these endeavors will not only enhance your skill set but also empower you to navigate the challenges and seize the opportunities that lie ahead in the world of multifamily.

To thrive in the long term, sponsors must also prioritize resident experience and community-building initiatives. In a competitive market, fostering a sense of community within properties can differentiate them from other offerings. Hosting social events, providing communal spaces, and maintaining transparent, responsive communication channels can significantly improve tenant retention rates. Happy tenants are more likely to renew leases, which in turn stabilizes occupancy and enhances the property's reputation.

As we close this guide, I encourage you to embrace the multifaceted nature of multifamily asset management with a balanced perspective: equal parts, discipline and persistence. This field offers unique opportunities but also presents distinct challenges, from mastering financial metrics to managing tenant relationships and adapting to market fluctuations. Your career in multifamily may be marked by hurdles and learning curves, yet each stage will build your expertise and deepen your understanding of what it takes to succeed. The complexities you'll encounter will refine your skills and resilience, preparing you to handle both the routine demands and unexpected shifts of a dynamic market.

As you move forward, remember that success is not defined solely by numbers on a balance sheet but by the tangible value you create within communities and the quality of life you help create for residents. Approach each task with a mindset focused on long-term impact—building stable, thriving living environments that not only enhance your property's reputation but also contribute to lasting value for investors. With a commitment to ongoing learning, discipline, and ethical stewardship, you'll find that the rewards of this work extend beyond financial gains. Embrace the journey, continuously refine your strategies, and strive to leave a meaningful mark on the multifamily real estate landscape.

If you've enjoyed the content of *THE APARTMENT PLAYBOOK, 24-YEARS OF INSIDER SECRETS*, I'd love to hear your feedback! Reviews help improve the work and can assist others in deciding whether to explore the book.

Feel free to share your thoughts on the following aspects:

- **Content clarity:** Was the information presented clearly and understandably?
- **Relevance:** Did the chapters address the key topics you were interested in?
- **Practical application:** Were the case studies and examples helpful in illustrating the concepts?
- **Overall experience:** What did you like most about the book, and what could be improved?

Your insights would be invaluable in refining future editions and helping other readers!

May your journey in multifamily industry be filled with growth, resilience, and rewarding success.

CASE STUDY

GLOSSARY

1031 Exchange (1031): A 1031 Exchange, named after Section 1031 of the IRS tax code, allows investors to defer paying capital gains taxes on the sale of investment properties by reinvesting the proceeds in a like-kind property.

Accredited Investor: An accredited investor is an individual or entity that meets certain financial criteria defined by the SEC, allowing them to invest in certain high-risk, high-return opportunities like private equity or hedge funds.

Bad Debt: Bad debt refers to the amount of rent or other income that is uncollectible from tenants, often due to defaults or vacancies.

Basis Point Spread (BPS): A basis point is one-hundredth of a percentage point (0.01%).

Cash on Cash (COC): Cash on cash return measures the annual return earned on the actual cash invested in a property. It is calculated by dividing the annual pre-tax cash flow by total cash investment.

CAP Rate (CAP): The capitalization rate (CAP rate) is the ratio of Net Operating Income (NOI) to the property's current market value. It is used to estimate the investor's return on a property if purchased with cash.

Capital Expenses (CapX): CapX refers to the funds used by a property owner to upgrade, and maintain physical assets like buildings, equipment, or renovations.

Debt Service Coverage Ratio (DSCR): This ratio measures the property's ability to cover debt obligations. It is calculated by dividing the NOI by the total debt service (principal and interest payments).

Department of Housing and Urban Development (HUD): HUD is a U.S. government agency responsible for overseeing housing policies, including affordable housing programs, and ensuring fair housing practices.

Effective Gross Income (EGI): EGI is the total income generated by a property, including rental income and other income, minus vacancy and collection losses.

Environmental Site Assessment (ESA): An ESA is a report that identifies potential or existing environmental contamination liabilities on a property, usually required before acquiring real estate.

General Partnership (GP): A general partnership refers to the managing entity in a real estate investment deal. The general partner is responsible for managing the day-to-day operations, decision-making, and overall management of the property, as well as bearing the most liability.

Geographic Information Systems (GIS): GIS refers to the technology used for spatial and geographical analysis, frequently used in real estate to analyze property locations, demographics, and other spatial data.

Gross Potential Rent (GPR): GPR is the maximum amount of rental income that a property could generate if all units were rented at market rates, with no vacancies.

Internal Rate of Return (IRR): This is the annual growth rate an investment is expected to generate. It considers the time value of money and provides a comprehensive view of the investment's profitability over time.

Interest Only (IO): An interest-only loan allows the borrower to pay only interest for a specified period, usually at the beginning of the loan term, with principal payments starting later.

Lease Rent Optimization (LRO): LRO refers to software that adjusts rental rates daily based on market demand and the property's current availability.

Letter of Intent (LOI): A LOI is a non-binding document that outlines the basic terms and conditions of a potential deal before the final purchase agreement is signed. It signals the intention to pursue a transaction.

Limited Liability Company (LLC): Offers liability protection and flexible management options.

Limited Partnership (LP): A limited partnership is a type of partnership where limited partners contribute capital but do not take part in the day-to-day operations. They have limited liability, meaning their risk is limited to the amount of capital they invest.

Loan to Cost (LTC): LTC is the ratio of the loan amount to the total cost of the project, including acquisition, renovation, and construction costs.

Loan to Value (LTV): LTV is the ratio of a loan amount to the appraised value of the property. It helps determine the risk level for the lender.

Loss/Gain to Lease (LTL): LTL is the difference between the contracted rent in place and the market rent. A positive LTL (gain) means the lease is above-market rent, and a negative LTL (loss) means the lease is below market rent.

Net Operating Income (NOI): NOI represents a property's total income after deducting operating expenses but before paying any mortgage or capital expenditures.

Offering Memorandum (OM): An OM is a Broker generated document provided to potential buyers that details information about an investment opportunity, including financials, and market analysis.

Pari-Passu: This term means "equal footing," where investors are treated equally in receiving returns or distributions proportional to their investment amounts.

Per Unit Per Year (PUPA): PUPA is a metric used to measure expenses on a per-unit-per-year basis, often used in multifamily property analysis.

Purchase Price (PP): PP refers to the total amount paid for a property.

Purchase and Sale Agreement (PSA): A PSA is a legal contract outlining the terms and conditions agreed upon by the buyer and seller for the transfer of a property.

Rent Roll (RR): A Rent Roll is a report that lists all the tenants of a property, their lease terms, rent amounts, and any outstanding balances.

Resident Utility Billing System (RUBS): RUBS is a method of allocating utility costs to tenants based on factors like unit size, number of occupants, or usage.

Return on Investment (ROI): The initial equity investment return after capital and ownership expenses.

Tenants in Common (TIC): A TIC is a form of ownership in which two or more parties hold undivided fractional interests in a property. Each party can sell, transfer, or will their ownership interest independently. This structure allows each tenant to continue to operate as an independent entity for the forward-looking or incoming investment of a 1031 Exchange.

Trailing 12 Months (T12): T12 refers to the financial performance of a property over the last 12 months. It provides a historical look at income and expenses.

Year to Date (YTD): YTD refers to the period starting from the beginning of the current calendar year up to the present date, often used to track financial performance or metrics for a property or portfolio.

Yield to Cost (YTC): YTC is a metric that compares the NOI to the total project cost. It is used to estimate an investor's return on a development or renovation project.

ABOUT THE AUTHOR

I am Baron Saterbak, and I have over two decades of experience in multifamily operations, acquisitions, due diligence, renovation, and asset management. My journey in multifamily real estate began at a young age and is rooted in a family legacy of dedication, discipline, and innovation. Born in San Diego, California, my earliest memories include accompanying my father to multifamily properties and construction job sites of multifamily properties, where I was introduced to the fundamentals of development and operations. These formative experiences laid the groundwork for my passion for the industry and instilled a deep respect for hard work and responsibility.

My grandfather, a brick mason, began developing single-family homes and subdividing lots in Southern California. After moving our family to Northwest Indiana, my father worked for a development company called Gough and Gough, expanding his architectural expertise into the historic tax credit reuse and large-scale developments across multiple states. These years shaped my understanding of the intricacies and challenges of development and entitlements.

As a teenager, I learned the invaluable role tenants play in a property's success. Pulling quarters from laundry machines wasn't just a task, it was an opportunity to interact with the tenants who were the heart of our properties. Whether it was greeting residents by name or understanding their concerns, I quickly realized that happy tenants are the foundation of a thriving property. These experiences, coupled with winter mornings spent alongside my father in a snowplow maintaining Midwest properties, taught me that real estate ownership is more than a financial investment. It's a hands-on responsibility, requiring unwavering commitment to both the physical asset and the people who call it home especially when stewarding investor capital.

My education extended beyond the classroom. Summers spent working for an architect in Northwest Indiana honed my skills in architectural design. One memorable summer, I designed a townhouse development alongside my father, only to discover he had submitted my plans to the planning commission and named the street after me. That gesture was a profound reminder of my father's trust and pride in my contributions.

The 2008 crash was an educational chapter in my life. A 440-unit condo conversion project began with record-breaking sales and became a textbook case of navigating a collapsing market, leaving a broken condo complex. The lessons learned during that period were invaluable, underscoring the importance of risk management and ensuring a project's timeline aligns with market realities. Don't get caught up in the wave. Sometimes, selling early is better than waiting too long. In the years that followed, I started over, taking on the reposition of a 312-unit property in Michigan. I lived the business plan—handling renovations, managing leasing standards, bidding contracts, and maintaining financial and investor relations.

I spent part of my early career at Axiom Properties in Lincolnshire, Illinois, a large value add multifamily owner. That tenure provided a solid and invaluable foundation for procedural and operational excellence. These experiences shaped my conservative approach to underwriting and long-term stability in asset management. When I returned to help build and oversee Bear Holdings Group's portfolio, I found that applying Midwestern methods to our growing portfolio reinforced my belief that operational integrity, utmost respect for the value of our tenants, and transparency, are paramount in multifamily ownership. It's easy for people to make money when rents go up 5+% a year, and management companies look like heroes in a rising tide market. The authentic operators show their true stripes in the valleys.

In this book, I aim to provide my readers with a comprehensive guide to multifamily asset management, from underwriting to disposition, by relying on my extensive experience and deep industry knowledge. Through a detailed case study, practical insights, and actionable strategies, I look to empower you to make informed investment decisions and succeed in the multifamily real estate market.

REFERENCES

A relatively brief history of development in Phoenix. (n.d.). Local First Arizona. https://localfirstaz.com/news-blog/a-brief-history-of-development-in-phoenix-and-a-briefer-look-ahead

Adam, K. (2024, July 11). *The top 6 landlord-friendly states of 2024.* LawDepot. https://www.lawdepot.com/landlord-friendly-states/

Adams, A. (2021, June 29). *Tenant screening policies to avoid fair housing violations.* Bay Property Management Group. https://www.baymgmtgroup.com/blog/tenant-screening-avoid-fair-housing-violations/

Chen, J. (2020, November 30). *What is an occupancy rate? Definition and use in analysis.* Investopedia. https://www.investopedia.com/terms/o/occupancy-rate.asp

From the Desk of Warren Buffett. (2024). Intelligent Im. https://www.intelligentim.com/from-the-desk-of-warren-buffet

Hollstein, F. (2020). Estimating beta: The international evidence. *Journal of Banking & Finance*, *121*, 105968. https://doi.org/10.1016/j.jbankfin.2020.105968

Iancu, T. (2024, April 2). *How to calculate DSCR (Debt Service Coverage Ratio) in commercial real estate.* CommercialEdge. https://www.commercialedge.com/blog/how-to-calculate-dscr-debt-service-coverage-ratio-in-commercial-real-estate/

Louisiana Realtors. (2022). *Why the Fair Housing Act is so important.* Louisiana Realtors. https://www.larealtors.org/blog/why-the-fair-housing-act-is-so-important

Trailing 12 months definition and explanation. (2022, August 26). Multifamily Loans. https://www.multifamily.loans/trailing-twelve-months/

Made in the USA
Monee, IL
04 November 2026

67384586R00125